THE
REFERENCE
SHELF

THE FARM CRISIS

HD
1761
.F27
1987

edited by ROBERT EMMET LONG

THE REFERENCE SHELF

Volume 59 Number 6

THE H. W. WILSON COMPANY

New York   1987

THE REFERENCE SHELF

The books in this series contain reprints of articles, excerpts from books, and addresses on current issues and social trends in the United States and other countries. There are six separately bound numbers in each volume, all of which are generally published in the same calendar year. One number is a collection of recent speeches; each of the others is devoted to a single subject and gives background information and discussion from various points of view, concluding with a comprehensive bibliography. Books in the series may be purchased individually or on subscription.

Library of Congress Cataloging in Publication Data

Main entry under title:

The Farm crisis / edited by Robert Emmet Long.

   p. cm. — (The Reference shelf ; v. 59, no. 6)
   A collection of reprints of previously published articles.
   Bibliography: p.
   1. Agriculture—Economic aspects—United States. 2. Agriculture and state—United States. I. Long, Robert Emmet. II. Series.
HD1761.F27 1987   338.1'0973—dc19   87-32159
ISBN 0-8242-0753-X

Printed in the United States of America

CONTENTS

PREFACE

The 1970s were boom years for American agriculture. During this period of rising production and increasing sales abroad, farmers were urged by then Secretary of Agriculture Earl Butz to plant from "fencerow to fencerow." They were encouraged to buy new farm equipment and acquire more land. Interest rates were relatively low, and these investments seemed sound since indebtedness would be offset by increased revenues. But at the beginning of the 1980s, the bottom began to drop out of American agriculture. Partly because Third World nations had overextended their borrowing credit and were then forced to reduce their imports, more crops were produced than could be sold. Land prices fell sharply, diminishing the collateral for loans assumed by farmers, and interest rates soared. The result in many cases was bankruptcy and the foreclosure of family farms. Since 1981 150,000 farms have been lost; nearly 43,000 in 1985 alone.

The focus of the farm crisis debate has been the medium-sized family farm, a unit more endangered than the large farm, which remains profitable, or the "rural residence," which does not provide the sole or even the chief source of income for its owners. It is the family farm that has borne the brunt of hardship in an often bitter struggle for survival. Economic analysts sometimes ask "Can the family farm be saved?" The answer, in the view of many, is that regardless of what legislation is passed there will be fewer of such farms in the future. Responses to the farm dilemma have varied. The Reagan administration, burdened by a huge budget deficit, would like to cut back its outlay of multibillion-dollar farm subsidies and to bring agriculture into line with a competitive "market-oriented" economy. But many farm organizations have strongly opposed such efforts. The 1985 Farm Bill, attempting to accommodate both the administration and the farmers, has not reversed the downward slide of farm income or the cost of federal spending, and new bills are now before Congress.

This compilation examines the farm crisis in its social, economic, and political aspects. The first section treats the situation of the farmer in various parts of the country. The opening article focuses on Iowa, perhaps the hardest hit of all the farm states, while others report on conditions elsewhere. The following section deals with the effect of hard times on farm communities, with their dwindling populations, crisis centers, rising suicide rates, and other evidence of great personal distress. The third section is concerned with the sources of the farm crisis, and includes an article from *Science* magazine that reveals how and why American farm commodities have suffered in the international market of the 1980s. In the final section various proposals for reshaping American agriculture are presented, together with different bills before Congress that address this complex and baffling problem.

The editor is indebted to the authors and publishers who have granted permission to reprint the materials in this compilation. Special thanks are due to the Fulton Public Library and to the staff of Penfield Library, State University of New York at Oswego.

ROBERT EMMET LONG

December 1987

I. HARD TIMES FOR THE FAMILY FARM

EDITOR'S INTRODUCTION

Agriculture is the nation's largest industry—larger than steel and automobile manufacture combined—and accounts for 20 percent of the Gross National Product. When hard times come to the farms, therefore, it is a source of concern for the entire country. According to one estimate, as many as 20 percent of the country's farmers may lose their livelihoods before the present crisis in agriculture can be contained—a disturbing projection of economic and human cost. Moreover, the affected areas are not limited to one region of the country. The Midwest, a major producer of grains, has suffered dramatically; in Iowa, for example, farm incomes have dipped 55 percent since the beginning of the 1980s. But the Great Plains and far Western states are also in difficulty, and the crisis has extended even to California which, because of its fertile soil and diversification of produce, had seemed impervious to market fluctuations.

Section I examines conditions for the family farmer in all of these regions. It begins with an article by Gregg Easterbrook from *Atlantic* magazine that focuses on Iowa. The following article from *The Progressive* recounts the struggle of small farmers in Wisconsin and their frustrating relations with the Farmers Home Administration, an agency originally intended to assist them. Finally, another report, from *The Christian Century*, describes the dwindling prospects of farmers in Missouri.

MAKING SENSE OF AGRICULTURE[1]

Americans are inclined to think of a crisis as a shortage, but agriculture is in crisis because of surpluses—too much of a good

[1]Reprint of an article by Gregg Easterbrook, *Atlantic* staff writer. Originally published in the July 1985 Atlantic Monthly. Copyright © 1985 by Gregg Easterbrook. Reprinted with permission.

thing. Farmers in the United States produce more food than their countrymen need or want; and although they do not produce as much as the hungry world needs, they produce far more than it can afford to buy. This has been the case ever since the Depression. Indeed, overproduction was a problem even during the Depression, and it has become unusually pronounced in the 1980s, as many Western countries and even a few developing nations have joined the United States in growing more food than anyone knows what to do with. The result is a tragedy of plenty, which offends many of our deepest convictions about resources, virtue, and the soil. One way or another, most of the confusion in American agricultural policy today arises from our reluctance to accept the idea that growing food is sometimes the wrong thing to do.

Few economic endeavors have any aura of romance and tradition. We don't get misty at the sight of a chain store framed against a prairie landscape or take comfort in knowing that each morning thousands of lawyers head out into the predawn darkness to tend their lawsuits. Farming, though, occupies an honored place in our culture. Even big-city sophisticates who would sooner die than attend a Grange Hall dance find it reassuring to know that somewhere out there honest folk are working the earth much as it has been worked for centuries.

Agricultural industries, from farming itself to the retailing of farm products, constitute the largest sector of the American economy, accounting for 20 percent of the GNP and employing more people than the steel and automobile industries combined. Yet many people find it heartless and somewhat unfair for anyone to speak of farming as an industry subject to the logic of supply and demand. To this sentimental faction the thought that any farmer should have to go out of business seems intolerable. As the cost of federal agricultural subsidies has risen, there has come into being an opposing faction, which dismisses farmers as spoiled welfare dependents who bilk the public on an unprecedented scale. Last winter's campaign for an emergency farm-credit bill seemed to divide politicians and the press into two camps: those who would "give 'em whatever they want" and those who would "let 'em fry."

The actual circumstances of modern farming conform to few if any of the assumptions that underlie the public debate. In order to see what condition American agriculture is in, one must first dispatch a number of widely held misconceptions.

—Farm families as a group are not poor. Their average income in 1983, one of the worst years in memory for agriculture, was $21,907. The average income for all families was $24,580. If one takes into account the lower costs of living in rural areas, farmers live about as well as other Americans. In fact, in some recent years farmers earned more than the national average.

—Farmers are not being driven from the land. From October of 1984 through January of 1985—when what was said to be a dire emergency for farmers was making news—the Farmers Home Administration actually foreclosed on forty-two farms nationwide. The FmHA provides loans to farmers who can't get credit elsewhere. Over the same four-month period its borrowers who "discontinued farming due to financial difficulties"—a broad category that reflects foreclosures by lienholders, bankruptcies, and voluntary liquidations to avert bankruptcy—totaled 1,249, or 0.5 percent of the FmHA's 264,000 clients.

From January to September of 1984 production-credit associations and federal land banks under the aegis of the Farm Credit Administration (which is much larger than the FmHA, handling about a third of U.S. agricultural debt) actually foreclosed on 2,908 loans nationwide. If one includes bankruptcies and loans in the process of liquidation, a total of 1.6 percent of FCA-aided farmers were in trouble.

Debt problems are real: early this year the FmHA, FCA-backed institutions, and rural farm banks saw delinquency rates reach record highs. But the incidence of dispossessions has been vastly exaggerated. The number of delinquent loans usually peaks early in the year, because most FmHA loans come due in January. Newspapers rarely follow up their winter reports of a "dramatic increase" in the number of farms in trouble with summer reports of a dramatic decline.

—Farming is not a disastrous investment. Farm lobbyists don't like to talk about disposable income, preferring to speak of "profit"—a problematic concept when applied to the self-employed, who can treat as business expenses items like vehicles and real estate, which most others must pay for out of their salaries. In 1983 and 1984 a trillion dollars' worth of farm assets generated a profit of $48 billion—an average return of 2.4 percent a year. But the annual net return on all corporate assets for the same period was only 5.5 percent.

—The "farm exodus" has been over for years. Much is made of the fact that the number of U.S. farms declined by 33,000 in 1982 and by 31,000 in 1983. But the declines were far bigger in the 1950s and 1960s—a period enshrined in political mythology as better for farmers. In 1951 the number of farms declined by 220,000; in 1956 by 140,000; in 1961 by 138,000.

—Agribusiness does not dominate farming. Only three percent of all U.S. farms are owned by corporations. Moreover, farm ownership is not becoming increasingly concentrated. About one percent of all owners of farmland hold 30 percent of farm acreage, but that ratio is the same as it was in 1946.

—Most agricultural products are not eligible for federal support. Federal programs concentrate on what are called basic crops—grains, cotton, rice, and dairy products. Fruits, vegetables, livestock, and specialty crops, such as nuts and garlic, are not subsidized. In recent years these products have often done better than the ones the government takes an interest in—a circumstance that some commentators view as proof that abolishing government programs would solve agriculture's problems. Right now, however, the two categories of farm products are in about the same depth of trouble.

—Most farmers don't get subsidies. Participation in the basic crop-subsidy programs is voluntary, and most farmers stay away. A study released in 1984 by the Senate Budget Committee found that the major subsidy programs covered only 21 percent of farms and 16.5 percent of farm acreage.

Those whose response to the increasing cost of agricultural programs is that we should continue the subsidies for small farmers but prevent large farmers from enjoying them should take note that the programs already function pretty much that way. The Senate Budget Committee study found that the largest farms were the least likely to be enrolled in subsidy programs. The most direct cash subsidy, called deficiency payments, is capped at $50,000 per farm per year, which renders the program of little value to large operations. Indeed, the one percent of owners controlling 30 percent of American farm acreage received only seven percent of the deficiency payments in 1983, and almost none of the FmHA and Small Business Administration benefits.

—No one can get rich on federal subsidies. While a very large amount of money is spent subsidizing U.S. agriculture, it is spread so thin that few individual farmers receive significant amounts.

Indiana farmers averaged $1,323 in federal cash payments in 1982; Kansas farmers averaged $1,577; figures in the rest of the heartland were about the same. In Arizona, where farmers receive by far the highest subsidies in the country, direct payments averaged $27,040. Farmers benefit from a variety of other subsidies, the per capita amounts of which are difficult to calculate but clearly not lavish.

—Most farmers don't have burdensome debt. President Reagan was wrong to say that "around four percent at best" of farmers need credit help, but the actual figure is not much higher. According to a study by the U.S. Department of Agriculture (USDA) which farm-spending advocates often cite, only 6.5 percent of all farmers are actually insolvent or on the verge of being so. The Federal Reserve System estimates that eight percent of farmers have debt-asset ratios over 70 percent, and another 11 percent have debt-asset ratios of 41 to 70 percent. But nearly 58 percent of all farmers are well in the clear, with debt-asset ratios of 10 percent or less.

From the impersonal standpoint of economics, the 19 percent of farmers who, according to the Federal Reserve, are in credit trouble might be viewed as representing agriculture's excess production capacity. Last year 81 percent of the production capacity of all U.S. industries was in use, leaving 19 percent idle. Looked at this way, the share of borderline cases in farming is not particularly different from that in other industries.

—Debt has hit farmers hard but not that hard. From 1974 to 1984 outstanding agricultural debt rose 193 percent. Through the same period consumer credit rose 172 percent, mortgage debt rose 167 percent, and all commercial bank debt rose 153 percent.

—The embargo on grain sales to the Soviet Union did not clobber wheat farmers. In 1980, the year the embargo was in full effect, agricultural exports jumped from $31 billion to $40 billion—the largest increase ever. Wheat exports increased from 1,375 million bushels in 1979 to 1,514 million in 1980 and increased again in 1981, to 1,771 million bushels. In 1982 and 1983, after the embargo was lifted, wheat exports declined.

Just Enough to Be Miserable

Farm groups, from the radical American Agriculture Movement to the rock-ribbed conservative American Farm Bureau
Federation, condemn federal agriculture programs as a matter of
ritual, and nearly every congressional hearing on agriculture
commences with a rendition of how horribly the government
treats the farmer. This is partly because agricultural programs
are a philosophical jumble. Containing elements of free-market
risk and federal bailouts, capitalist entrepreneurship and socialist
central planning, they do not reinforce anyone's world view.

Consumers might say, Don't knock success. U.S. agriculture
not only produces an abundance of nutritious food but does so
at low consumer prices. Americans spend a smaller percentage of
their disposable income on food than do the citizens of any other
industrial nation; in the past ten years, as the Consumer Price Index has risen by 114 percent, supermarket prices have risen by
only 96 percent. Even when the cost of subsidies—which consumers must pay too, through their taxes—is taken into account,
food remains cheap. If the roughly $21 billion being spent in this
fiscal year to subsidize agriculture were reflected directly in consumer costs, supermarket prices would be only about six percent
higher than they are.

Some farmers dislike federal programs because they don't
want the government interfering with their lives, and others dislike the programs because they wish the government would inter-
fere more. The range of opinion is not hard to understand. Farm
subsidies provide just enough money to keep nearly every farmer
in business producing just enough excess supply to hold prices
down. This means that farmers who depend on government subsidies will find it hard to become prosperous enough to do without them. It also means that farmers who aren't subsidized get
lower prices than they would if no one was subsidized. Everybody
works, but everybody is miserable.

The main subsidy programs are deficiency payments and
loans, both of which are administered by the Commodity Credit
Corporation. Deficiency payments are straightforward. The farmer simply gets in the mail a check for the difference between the
market price and a target price, which is set by Congress. A CCC
loan is more involved. A farmer borrows a sum calculated by the
government to reflect the value of his crop, and he puts up the

crop itself as collateral. The loan is like a salary. If the market prices turns out to be higher than the loan rate, the farmers can sell the crop, satisfy the loan, and keep the premium. If the market price is not higher than the loan rate, the farmer activates a "nonrecourse clause" and turns over the crop—the collateral—to close out his obligation. In effect he has forced the government to buy his product.

The cost of agriculture subsidies is difficult to predict. For example, when the farm bill expiring this year (which covers almost all agriculture subsidies) was passed in 1981, its cost was estimated at $11 billion. Because lawmakers assumed that inflation, running hot in 1981, would continue through the lifetime of the bill, they programmed in large annual increases in loan rates and target prices. Instead inflation cooled, the recession held agricultural exports down, market prices wavered, and loan rates and target prices ended up being higher in relation to market prices than expected. As a result, instead of a total of $11 billion since 1981 the legislation has cost $53 billion. This fiscal year alone the outlay for CCC purchasers and deficiency payments is expected to reach $14.2 billion.

In theory the subsidy system combats overproduction, because farmers who "seal" their crops with the CCC must agree to leave idle a percentage of their acreage. But in practice it can backfire. Eligibility is based on acreage: the more acres a farmer has available for production, the more generous his subsidy can be. Thus farmers sodbust land neither needed nor efficient, solely to get credit for the acreage. And nothing in the program prevents farmers from increasing production, by using more fertilizers, pesticides, and machinery, on land they are not required to idle. It is not unusual for a farm's output to go up in a year in which acreage has been set aside to please the CCC.

Next in dollar value are subsidized loans from the Farmers Home Administration. In this fiscal year the FmHA is spending about $3 billion for below-market operating loans (loans that pay for seed, fertilizer, and so on). Originally the FmHA was to provide only temporary assistance, but now many recipients stay in the system year after year. (When the first federal price-support program was created, in 1933, the secretary of agriculture, Henry Wallace, called it a "temporary method of dealing with an emergency." The emergency farm-credit bill that monopolized the attention of Congress early this year was, like most agricultural assistance, portrayed as a one-time extraordinary measure. There was also an emergency farm-credit bill in 1984, and, barring some miracle, there will have to be another in 1986.)

FmHA assistance is available only to farmers who have already been turned down by commercial banks or production-credit associations. The 264,000 farmers kept in business by the FmHA represent only 11 percent of a total 2.4 million. Yet 11 percent can make all the difference in the marketplace. For example, in commodity markets like those for grain, oil, and gold, where products have no distinguishing features and only numbers count, often the final few percentage points—what economists call the marginal supply—sway the price for all producers. OPEC's Arab members set world oil prices for almost a decade though they produced about a third of the world's oil. Oil was in tight supply, it was a seller's market, and all oil became worth what OPEC was charging, because any seller knew that he could find a buyer willing to pay the marginal price. Now there is a buyer's market for oil, and the OPEC price can no longer be enforced.

Likewise, in 1972, the year of the first major Russian grain purchase (the "Great Grain Robbery"), U.S. wheat prices zoomed from $1.76 a bushel to $3.95. The Russian acquisition totaled just 22 percent of the wheat available on U.S. markets that year, and by December there was more surplus grain in our stockpiles than the Soviets had bought. But the marginal supply had been carried away and the market converted from a buyer's to a seller's domain. By the same token, a moderate percentage of extra supply can depress prices, by robbing sellers (farmers) of their bargaining leverage. In 1981, for example, the corn harvest increased by 22 percent while domestic consumption and exports—or, as the USDA calls it, total "disappearance"—declined slightly. As a result, corn prices fell from $3.11 a bushel to $2.50.

Overproduction becomes acute in the basic crop categories, because one year's mistakes are stored and added to those of the next. In 1981 U.S. fields produced a record 15.6 million bales of cotton, but only 11.8 million "disappeared." Leftovers from 1981 have been plaguing the cotton market ever since. In 1983, for example, cotton production was down to 7.7 million bales and demand was up to 12.7 million, but because the year began with eight million bales in storage, cotton supply still exceeded demand by almost 25 percent. Today the price of cotton is about what it was in 1976, with no adjustment for inflation, and it's below what some growers spend on production.

When foreign demand falls off, the cumulative effects of overproduction become especially painful. Roughly four out of ten acres are planted for foreign sale. Since the early 1970s wheat producers have been serving the foreign market first and the U.S. market as a sideline; in the record years of 1980 and 1981 twice as many bushels were shipped overseas as were used at home. If foreign customers fail to buy, as has lately been the case, there's nowhere for the crops to go but into storage, because the United States already has all the food it needs. Even drastic price cuts would produce at best only a slight increase in U.S. consumption (food generally being subject to what economists call inelastic demand: most buyers want about the same amount regardless of variations in price). Soybean growers produced 2,035 million bushels last year and sold 1,880 million, leaving 155 million in silos. Export demand, which had peaked at 929 million bushels in 1981, was down to 800 bushels. Had export demand stayed at the 1981 level, 1984 would have been a banner year for soybean farming; instead the price of soybeans fell from $7.75 to $6.60 a bushel, and concern about the surplus hangs over this year's planting.

Next on the list of federal subsidies is $954 million for soil and water conservation. The same federal policies that encourage sodbusting of questionable land and boosting production by means of chemicals are to blame for a significant portion of the erosion that this subsidy is meant to control. Another $421 million goes to subsidize federal crop insurance, and about $350 million is spent on emergency loans to help FmHA farmers whose crops have been damaged by weather.

An extra $24.3 million in direct subsidies to farmers was provided in 1984 by the Small Business Administration, under a program that issues cut-rate loans to those hit by natural disasters. (In 1984 SBA "nonphysical-disaster" loans were granted to fertilizer companies in states where commodities released under the payment-in-kind program had reduced demand for fertilizer—one federal subsidy chasing another.) Agriculture also benefits indirectly from the $1.1 billion spent on farm research and extension services, the $18.2 billion spent on food stamps and child-nutrition programs, and the $1.8 billion in Food for Peace aid to poor countries, all of which shore up crop demand. Finally, many billions have been spent on federally subsidized irrigation and electrical power in the West. For a variety of reasons, the exact cost of these subsidies—beyond $80 million being spent this year to subsidize two- and five-percent loans for power and telephone lines to rural communities—defies calculation. Much of the expense is coming to an end, however, because of a law passed in 1982 that requires western growers to begin paying the full cost of their water.

It is common for farmers—and reporters—to speak as if in a just society virtuous products like food and fiber would only increase in value. Yet we find nothing amiss when the price of computers or eyeglasses falls, and we're upset when the prices of energy and housing climb. A successful economy is supposed to drive down the prices of goods, especially manufactured goods— and the advent of fertilizers, pesticides, self-propelled combines, and large tractors has made agriculture one of the least labor-intensive of industries. Each year the USDA charts farming "inputs" for capital and labor. The 1980 input for farm labor was a fifth that of 1930, while the input for machinery was three times greater, and the input for chemicals was twenty times greater. Farm groups say that there is something wrong with the fact that wheat costs less in real terms today than it did in 1870. There would be something wrong if it *didn't* cost less.

Farm-state congressmen often cite the index of prices for farm products from the Producer Price Index kept by the Bureau of Labor Statistics. The PPI, like the Consumer Price Index, uses 1967 as its base year. Whereas the CPI rose to 311 in 1984, the index of prices for farm products has risen only to 256. The congressmen never mention that the indexes for almost *every* commodity within the PPI are behind, or only equal to, the CPI. Textile products and apparel are at 210, furniture and household appliances at 219, and rubber and plastic products at 247. Only non-metallic mineral products, at 337, and energy, at 657, are significantly ahead of the CPI. For that matter, low producer prices keep the cost of running a farm down. Indeed, according to the USDA, the index of what machines, supplies, interests, taxes, and wages cost farmers runs about ten percent below the rate of inflation.

No one likes to be thought of as being on the federal dole, least of all farmers, who put a premium on self-reliance. Farm groups across the spectrum invariably say, "We don't want subsidies, we just want a price," meaning higher market prices, and they note that higher prices would result in less federal spending, because deficiency payments would decline. The next logical step is usually not taken. Absent increased demand, higher prices can be realized only if excess production is controlled, either by cutting subsidies and letting some farmers fail (anathema to the left) or by imposing fierce restrictions on how much and what a farmer may plant (anathema to the right).

Farmers find it difficult to face the overproduction issue, mainly because of the nature of rural life. One of the salient cultural differences between farmers and city folk is that farmers live in places where everybody is in pretty much the same line of work. Everybody either is a farmer or provides a service that farmers need. Imagine if advertising executives had to live in complexes populated entirely by other advertising executives and could have only advertising executives for friends. Would they be so aggressive about stealing business? To be true capitalists, farmers would have to view their neighbors as their archenemies. So they compensate by viewing farming itself—the act of working the fields, not of selling the finished product—as their purpose and keeping everybody going as their political challenge. This thinking reflects the kindness and communal purpose we admire in rural life. It also makes for too many farmers.

The regular experience of shared achievement and sorrow in a common pursuit is among the most appealing aspects of rural tradition. Indeed, farm advocates often argue that the communal quality of rural America should be preserved for its own sake, even if economics has passed it by. They say that farm living sets a spiritual example whose worth thus transcends cost-benefit analysis. But when farmers say that their way of life should be preserved for its own sake, inevitably they must argue that all farmers are equally deserving of protection—that farmers have a right to remain farmers.

Iowa: Fellowship Replaced by Machinery

In an industry as large as American agriculture nothing is typical. There are the livestock pens of Texas, the vast irrigation networks of Nebraska and Arizona, the hog pens of Illinois and Indiana, the pastoral dairies of Wisconsin and Minnesota, the tiny tobacco plots of the mid-South, the citrus orchards of Florida, the uninterrupted wheat fields of Kansas. Nowhere is contrast more distinct than between the number-one and number-two agriculture states—California and Iowa.

California is a high-tech paradise. Farms are majestic; the climate is blissful. Californians produce some 200 commodities, including milk (the dairy business, surprisingly, is the state's biggest agriculture concern), cotton, rice, cattle, grapes, vegetables, plums, oranges, and almonds. Many farms are diversified: designed to produce several categories of crops and to shift from one to another as rapidly as demand changes.

In Iowa, farming is practiced more or less the way it always has been. Nearly all Iowa farms are family enterprises, and nearly all raise corn, soybeans, hogs, and cattle. The Iowa earth can be harsh, the weather cruel.

Just what constitutes a family farm of the Iowa variety depends on the beholder. A growing number of the nation's 2.4 million farmers—right now, roughly half—sell less than $10,000 worth of crops a year. Generally they work full-time jobs and farm on the side. According to Luther Tweeten, an agricultural economist at Oklahoma State University, most of these part-time farmers sell what they raise for less than they spend on production, leaving them several hundred to a thousand dollars in the hole each year, at least on paper. Such part-time farmers, Tweeten says, enjoy farming as an avocation and seek to qualify for farm tax breaks.

Those who sell from $40,000 to $100,000 worth of crops a year form the group commonly called family farmers. There are 381,000 of them, making up about 16 percent of the total farm population, and they are the most troubled—holding a disproportionate share of farm debt and typically having a lower disposable income than part-time farmers, because the farm is their sole source of income. Iowa is this group's stronghold.

The typical Iowa farmhouse is weathered beyond its years, with paint in various stages of peeling and cracks in interior walls. Visiting two dozen farms in various parts of the state last winter, I saw only one house that could qualify for teleportation to the middle-class suburbs of Atlanta or Portland—or Des Moines, for that matter. None of the farms I saw had paved driveways; several farmers who described themselves as successful mentioned as evidence of their good fortune gravel-covered drives. Owing to the lack of asphalt and concrete, mud was everywhere, deep enough in spots to make walking a trick.

Yet the people on these farms did not live in poverty. Nearly all the farmhouses I visited contained microwave ovens, color TVs, video-cassette recorders, and other tokens of consumer culture. No farmer I met drove a fancy car, but none lacked a car, either. All were well clothed and well fed. And the farm equipment that some possessed was a sight to behold: combines with wingspans like those of aircraft; four-wheel-drive tractors that could pull a Greyhound bus from a ditch; a few Steigers, the Corvettes of tractors, fitted out with air-conditioners and tape decks. This gleaming machinery, more than anything else, represents a profound change in the way farmers live—in the debt burdens they bear and in their relationships with their communities.

"Too many tractors with too much horsepower" is how Helen Lester, of Milo, who has been farming with her husband, Guy, since the Depression, summarized Iowa's predicament. Academics and journalists are not the only ones who began to believe around the mid-1960s that the small farm was doomed. Farmers believed it too. Awesome new tractors and combines would enable a family farmer to cultivate more land than ever. Farmers would almost have to buy more acres in order to spread those capital investments over a larger income base. Big new machines on bigger farms held out the promise that the family farmer could achieve the touted economies of scale enjoyed by sprawling ranches in Texas and the Southwest.

These machines also held out the promise of a more pleasant life, free of tedium and backbreaking labor. A Steiger, with its immense power, could plow more land in one day than a conventional tractor could plow in a week; the big combines would harvest crops with much less need for manpower. Improved seed varieties and chemicals were also coming into play, and were expected to diminish the demand that raising crops made on a farmer's time. What a dream began to emerge: a bigger farm, a higher income, and less physical work. The race was on. Sales of heavy machinery soared, and farms, even family farms, expanded in size.

The value of agricultural real estate escalated from $216 billion in 1970 to $756 billion in 1980 and then crashed. In 1984 it was $765 billion—a decline of about 23 percent when inflation is taken into account. In all the commentary on this fabulous rise and fall, it is rarely noted that farmers themselves were the driving force behind the price changes. Urban growth, often presented as the culprit, exerted a minor influence at best: only three percent of all land in the United States is built on, for cities, suburbs, or highways. When farmers sell, it is almost always to other farmers: the most prized farmland is that which adjoins an existing farm. Through the 1970s farmers sought more land, and farm size increased by an average of 13 percent.

Traditionally farmers have been frugal people, fearful of debt and wary of promises of quick wealth. But they did not respond to the economic developments of the 1970s with characteristic reserve. (In fairness, neither did millions of other Americans. Major corporations lost billions of dollars in sure-thing energy investments, and all sorts of people bought real estate as if the prices could never break, poising their loans on the assumption of perpetual inflation.) Using machines, chemicals, and new land, farmers both here and abroad expanded their productive capacity by so much in the 1970s that a fall became all but certain. Production through the decade rose at three percent a year in the United States, a record pace for annual growth. Meanwhile, food demand was not increasing as fast as production, and demand for some foods was falling.

Many farmers who bought large machinery told themselves that they would cover the payments by doing "custom work"—tilling and harvesting for other farms. As ownership of combines and 400-horsepower tractors became unremarkable, more farmers were offering custom work than needing it done. One farmer I visited, Pat Meade, in Milo, said, "You can pretty much tell which farms are in trouble by whether they're four-wheel or two-wheel." Meade uses a 1976 100-horsepower tractor that he maintains himself. He said, "When farmers discovered that a big machine would enable them to do all their plowing in a single day and spend the rest of the week at the coffee shop, a lot of them couldn't resist, even if they couldn't afford it. Combines were the worst. The average family farmer actually uses his combine less than thirty days a year. The rest of the time it sits in a shed. Seventy-five to a hundred thousand dollars sitting in your shed, doing nothing." Farmers who went heavily into debt to buy big machines and more acres were dubbed plungers.

A century ago the free-silver movement, led by William Jennings Bryan, centered on the desire for a liberal money supply so that there would be more for farmers to borrow and more for consumers to spend. In the 1970s inflation, though less glorious in conception than free silver, provided the financial climate many farmers had always thought they wanted. Plungers became community heroes. Farm journals were filled with stories of "young tigers" who were not afraid to take on staggering debt loads. "Those who dive deepest will come out on top" was a common saying. When briefly during the 1970s interest rates were below the inflation rate, borrowers came out ahead merely by borrowing. Farmers are dependent on credit even in good times, because they must pay production expenses months before they have crops to sell. The economic conditions of the 1970s seemed to say that it had actually become smart to pile loans on top of loans. But if inflation stopped, the loans would smash into each other like race cars trying to avoid a wreck.

The FmHA, production-credit associations, and banks were just as much to blame for plunging as farmers. With acreage values rising at up to 20 percent a year, farmland was an investment that was staying ahead of inflation. Many banks, needing borrowers to generate income on their inflation-pumped deposits, encouraged farmers to leverage themselves to the limit. According to Meade, "During the 1970s there were times when lenders quite literally drove up and down the road, knocked on people's doors, and asked them if they could use more credit." Philip Lehman, a farmer in Slater, Iowa, and an official of the Iowa Farmers Union, an organization that lobbies for increased federal farm aid, sat on the loan-approval board of a production-credit association in the early 1970s. "Things got to where it was difficult for me to put my initials on the applications," Lehman told me. "It was like granting people licenses to go under."

As inflation and gleaming supertractors dispelled farmers' qualms about extravagant spending, so they altered the spirit of farm communities. Farmers who drove Steigers didn't have to call on their neighbors for help when a wagon got stuck in the mud. Those with combines didn't have to wait for harvesting crews, nor did they have to offer to join in harvesting a neighbor's land. Many farmers borrowed to build their own silos and storage facilities during the 1970s, loosening their dependence on town silos and diminishing their obligation to attend co-op meetings. Farmers began to feel guilty of what they disliked most about city dwellers—an absence of community spirit.

"Because farmers want to be self-reliant, the combines and the tractors had an extremely seductive appeal," James Schutter, the pastor of the United Methodist church in Tingley, Iowa, told me last winter. "Machines made you really self-reliant. People didn't realize the machines would also make you isolated. As soon as it became technologically possible to farm independently, everybody wanted that." Milton Henderson, of Mt. Ayr, Iowa, who is retired after working for the Iowa State University extension service for thirty years, said, "Threshing and harvesting parties were wonderful events—much warmer, and more human, community events than the kind we have now, like high school basketball games." He added, "I would never want to go back to the past, plowing four acres a day with a team of horses. I'm just saying the sense of fellowship is gone, replaced by machinery."

Dairy, livestock, and poultry farmers still work year-round, because animals must be tended continually, but well-equipped crop farmers have it easier. They face three months of heavy work during planting and two more at harvest. Farm crisis stories tend to appear in winter partly because it is then that crop farmers, without daily work to do in their fields, do their lobbying. When the American Agricultural Movement staged its tractorcade in 1979, bringing hundreds of farm machines to Washington to block traffic, AAM members made speech after speech about how their backs were to the wall. Yet many had arrived in brand-new Steigers equipped with stereo systems, and some spent several months in the capital, in no apparent hurry to attend to their businesses. William Olmsted, a United Methodist minister in Greenfield, Iowa, has noticed a subtle change in farm sociology. He told me, "Making your rounds in winter, you could knock on doors at five farmhouses in a row and find no one home. They've gone to town, or are on vacation. Farmers used to *always* be home."

Fencerow to Fencerow

Farmers say they expanded in the 1970s because they were sent a signal from the highest levels of government instructing them to do so. There can be no doubt that they were.

In the 1970s the USDA predicted that food production would fall behind world demand. A book called *Famine 1975* attracted considerable attention when it was published in 1967. When the 1972 Russian grain deal caused wheat prices to rise and poor harvests caused food in general to become costlier, many thought that the pessimistic forecasts had been confirmed and they began to cry shortage. Richard Nixon's secretary of agriculture, Earl Butz, is said to have advised farmers to plant "from fencerow to fencerow." That phrase is now fixed in the heartland's litany of woes as firmly as the Russian grain embargo: farmers refer to it again and again. In 1973 the headline of an article in *The New York Times* declared, "Days of 'Cheap Food' May Be Over." As the decade passed and world harvests remained poor, the idea that the Russians and others would soon be begging us for grain caught hold. Oil prices were rising and the market for gasohol, made with corn alcohol, seemed about to take off. Declarations that agriculture was "the bulwark of democracy," "America's answer to OPEC," and so on became political clichés. When exports were booming, in 1980, President Jimmy Carter's secretary of agriculture, Bob Bergland, declared, "The era of chronic overproduction . . . is over."

"About ten years ago it looked like you just couldn't go wrong by expanding," Jim White, a farmer in Pleasantville, Iowa, told me. White is operating his farm under Chapter 11 of the federal bankruptcy code. In the late 1970s White bought land and equipment on credit and also co-signed notes so that two of his sons would be able to enter farming. In White's house a stack of foreclosure documents sits by trophies that White and his father won for being Polk County Corn Champions in 1963 and 1964. "My dad had taught me to be cautious, but everybody—I mean everybody—was saying that biggest had become best," White said.

Who in the 1970s could have predicted that by 1985 rising inflation would be only a memory, that the value of the dollar would rise so dramatically on the world exchange market, that developing countries would begin producing food for export, that gasohol would flop (gas stations in Iowa now post signs proclaiming NO ALCOHOL IN OUR FUEL), and that consumption of dairy products and red meat would decline? This web of events surprised even smooth-talking experts. The average farmer could not possibly have forseen it. White's production-credit-association loans contained variable-interest-rate clauses. "They said I had nothing to worry about—that rates had varied only a fraction of a point since 1970," White told me. "My rate went from 7 percent to 18.5 percent."

Does the fact that the government has misled farmers confer on them a right to special compensation? The frequency with which the national winds shift leads politicians routinely to give industries bad advice, and part of being a businessman is knowing what to ignore and what to take seriously. More important, though Earl Butz's advice certainly sounds foolish in today's economic climate, it was delivered thirteen years ago, in a different climate. How many businesses could survive by clinging to strategies thirteen years out of date? There would be scant public sympathy for an automobile company still making cars that get ten miles to a gallon. Because of the nature of agriculture, farmers have a more difficult time responding to economic changes than people in other industries. But this does not mean that they should be exempt from having to respond. In February the entire South Dakota state legislature traveled to Washington to lobby for more farm aid. When South Dakota's governor, William Janklow, appeared on the ABC News program *Nightline* to state his case, he absolved farmers of blame because, he said, "Earl Butz told them to plant fencerow to fencerow"—as though this had happened the year before.

It could be that farmers attach almost religious significance to what Butz said because it was the one time they were told exactly what they wanted to hear. Agriculture, a quiet line of work in which it was nearly impossible to get rich, was going to take off. Thanks to technology, incomes would rise and workloads would fall; farmers would rescue the country from foreign debt and become national heroes. With crops in demand, farmers could sell them on the market, not to the government, and make their money fair and square. Everything was finally going to be all right. It is human nature to cling to the moment when things were going to be all right, and so it is natural that farmers should cling to the vision of the early 1970s.

For farmers, government policy is like the weather. It's good for a spell, it's bad for a spell, and there's just no predicting. In addition to making business planning difficult, flip-flops of policy inevitably build resentment against government, even when the subsidies are flowing.

One farmer, in Creston, Iowa, told me, "I know for a fact that agriculture is controlled by a special committee of bankers and manufacturing interests and that no one is allowed to use the committee's name." Another, in Corydon, Iowa, said, "There was a secret meeting in 1947 at which a plan was laid out to destroy the family farm, and everything that has happened since comes directly from the plan." The two speakers were not kooks, and I heard similar sentiments from others during my travels in Iowa.

A fair reading of recent history is that the federal government would have to form a firing squad just to shoot itself in the foot. Nevertheless, some farmers do believe that their trouble must have a nefarious source. Many look outside the federal government. A popular target of suspicion is the Chicago Board of Trade, which most farmers resent as a rich man's plaything designed to make easy profits from the workingman's toil, and which some are convinced was invented by the anti-farm conspiracy in order to cause chaos in farm prices. (Some farmers now use the commodities exchange to hedge their crops, but the Iowa farmers I spoke to said they simply couldn't bring themselves to do that, even if it does make business sense.) Conspiracy theories in themselves are probably harmless, but their prevalence in rural communities suggests that farmers wish to fix the blame as far away from home as possible—to dwell in an unreal world. That wish helps to explain why farmers seem so bitter in television news footage.

Dissatisfaction rules life on the farm today, and the unhappiness farmers vent in the media or at political rallies probably does more to advance the idea of an endless crisis in farming than does the actual incidence of foreclosures. The unhappiness stems in part from raised and then dashed expectations. "Every year for the last fifty years had been a little better than the year before, until the 1980s," Carolyn Erb, a farmer in Ackworth, Iowa, said when I met with her last winter. At some point having a better year begins to seem like a right. That the Washington, D.C., tractorcade was staged in 1979, a year that turned out to be the second best on record for farm profit, shows how consuming a force self-pity can be.

The structure of farm economics guarantees that farmers will be frustrated. Suppose your year's salary would be $20,000, $40,000, or $60,000, with the amount determined by a lottery based on what day you asked for your pay. That is the arrangement that most farmers have to live with. The advent of international blockbuster deals adds turbulence to the market. "Now our decision on exactly what day to sell can make us or break us for the entire year," Nancy Meade told me.

Many businesses, of course, must deal with macroeconomic unknowns, but how many individual workers have to? Auto workers are not expected each time they report to their shift to perform an analysis of international sales patterns, according to which their wages will later be calculated. Family farmers must be laborers, market analysts, and financial managers all at once. Considering the modest track record of specialists who do nothing but predict agricultural markets, it is unreasonable to expect the records of individual farmers to be any better. The anxiety over when to sell can place extreme stress on a farm marriage: the husband may feel obligated to dictate the selling strategy, which offends the wife, who in turn blames the husband for market changes he couldn't possibly have predicted. The sheer uncertainty is oppressive. To return to the salary-lottery analogy, even if you picked the $60,000 day you would be upset about the wringer you'd been put through.

Endless waiting for Washington to make up its mind about farm programs produces more unhappiness. Ronald Reagan announced the latest emergency credit program for farmers in September, 1984, but as of February, 1985, with spring planting approaching, the FmHA had made decisions on only about two percent of the applications it had received. Farmers who had asked for aid had to sit and stew all fall and winter, wondering whether they would be able to stay in business and powerless to find out. Many of those who ultimately got extra help were inclined to be resentful rather than grateful.

Dissatisfaction extends even to successful farmers. Because federal subsidies have the effect of keeping everybody at least barely in business, overproduction prevents successful farmers from realizing the profits they otherwise might. Since farm commodities are basically interchangeable, farmers cannot compete with one another by offering different features or higher quality, as manufacturers can. They can compete only by undercutting already depressed market prices. Those who resisted taking the debt plunge or who run their operations unusually well say they feel pressured to pay for the errors of the careless.

Suppose the government stepped into the computer industry, which is suffering from oversupply, to make sure no manufacturer went out of business. Successful companies like IBM and Apple would be unhappy, because the artificial stimulation of supply would prevent them from getting full value for their products. Unsuccessful companies would find themselves in the debilitating position of being dependent on Uncle Sam and ridden with anxiety over whether their handouts would continue. Everyone would be working, yet no one would be happy. There would be a "computer crisis."

In farm communities across the heartland there is one more level of anxiety. Farmers have never been able to look forward to wealth, but they have had a satisfaction that city workers with better pay cannot hope for—the moment when they hand the farm over to their children. For many farmers that moment is the culmination of a responsible life; for the younger generation it is the moment when the world recognizes that they have done what was expected of them. "Right now it's not a responsible act to bring a son into the business, and you don't know what that does to the farmer's mind," Rod Erb, Carolyn's husband, told me. Transferring a highly capitalized farm from parent to child entails leveraging to the hilt. Under these circumstances parents consider themselves failures, and children, unable to do what generations before them have done, feel they have compromised their entire family histories.

After I left Iowa, there was one farm couple that I couldn't get out of my mind: Dennis and Patricia Eddy, who live in Stuart and have three young sons. The Eddys are existing on six subsidized loans. They had qualified for the Reagan emergency credit aid, which would save them about $23,000 in interest payments overall. They hadn't paid income taxes in five years. The kitchen of their farmhouse had been remodeled and was strikingly attractive; I noticed a microwave oven and other minor luxuries. They had a pure-bred Doberman puppy. Here was a couple who could easily be portrayed as hooked on handouts. "Just once in my life I would like to live at the poverty line," Patricia complained, yet her federal aid is more than many city families with greater need receive—to say nothing of the fact that she lives in her own home. Most urban welfare recipients, I felt sure, would exchange places with the Eddys in the blink of an eye.

Except for the kitchen, however, the Eddys' home was modest. By no stretch of the imagination was the family living indulgently. There didn't seem to be any chance that they would buy a sports car, eat in three-star restaurants, or enjoy many other luxuries that young professionals who went to graduate school on government-subsidized loans consider their due. I felt sure that none of the conservative theoreticians who rail against subsidies in the fastness of paneled libraries would exchange places with the Eddys.

The Eddys said that they were dismayed by having had six different FmHA loan supervisors in eighteen months, each of whom had issued a new set of instructions on how the couple ought to run their lives; by unending anxiety about whether their crops would grow and in turn sell; and by the public perception that those in debt to the FmHA are "bad farmers," which surely is not true.

For a while policymakers diagnosed increasing federal agricultural expenditures as a problem caused by "bad farmers" and "bad managers," who squandered their aid. The label has stuck—one farmer introduced himself to me as "just another bad manager"—although there is nearly universal agreement among agricultural observers that truly lazy or incompetent farmers are rare. If anything, farmers are *too* good at what they do. They produce too much and they are baffled and anguished by the fact that bringing food out of the ground, as they were taught was right, does not invariably lead to success. The Eddys were working as hard as they knew how, and that was what stayed with me.

California: MBAs in Overalls

Iowa seems like an outpost on the moon by comparison with the San Joaquin Valley, in central California. Nearly anything will grow in the valley's benign climate. The land is flat, which is perfect for farming, and cows graze in the nearby foothills in the Sierra Nevada as if they were in the Alps. In Iowa some farmers had plowed and planted their front yards, but here in Fresno and Tulare counties, one of the world's most productive agricultural regions, every square inch seemed to have been tilled. Farmhouses are modern ranch-style buildings with carports. Machinery doesn't rust. In the Midwest, farms are discrete places because farmers generally buy only land that adjoins their own; in California, however, farms tend to consist of scattered parcels. The scattering lowers the sentimental value of each farm, and it also works against any sense that farms are fortresses to be defended against an encroaching outside world. Farms in California seem much more like businesses. One sees few four-wheel-drive tractors with balloon tires. "Farmers like to buy tractors, managers like to make money," a Californian told me when I visited farms in the state last winter.

One of California's largest operations is Harris Farms, Inc., of Coalinga. The average U.S. farm has 437 acres; Harris has 17,000, and it's as diversified as can be—cotton, tomatoes, garlic, almonds, onions, grapes, potatoes, wheat, and cattle. It is not a corporate farm; John Harris, the only child of the founder, is the sole owner. During the 1970s, when the land frenzy drove prices to $3,500 an acre in the valley and as high as $15,000 an acre in the prestigious vineyard counties, Harris didn't buy. "We could never figure out how to make buying land at those prices pay," he told me.

Harris has 125 full-time workers, whom he calls "employees," and 100 units of housing for them, of a quality better than that of a trailer park but not as good as that of a subdivision. Unskilled seasonal laborers—migrant workers—make $4 an hour, full-time tractor operators make about $14,000 a year, and foremen make up to $65,000. Two foremen, Richard Lobmeyer and Juan Barrera, spend an increasing amount of time with computers: Harris Farms has a large mainframe computer for accounting and half a dozen personal computers for other tasks.

Barrera, for example, uses software designed for tomato growing to track temperature, humidity, and the rate of transpiration and to predict exactly how much irrigation the vines will need. Harris has been switching to less wasteful means of irrigation, such as drip pipes, which apply small doses of water directly to a plant's roots. (Before the 1982 law was passed, many heartland farmers complained bitterly that California water was subsidized, ignoring the fact that their own water falls from the sky free of charge.) Much of Harris's production is sold to food processors by a standard supplier's contract—a promise to deliver a certain tonnage of, say, tomatoes on a given day at an agreed price. This reduces the potential for a windfall, but it also eliminates anxiety over fluttering prices.

In rural communities it seems to be considered bad taste to build a luxurious house, and Harris does not flout that convention. He lives in the modest house where he was raised, which sits directly across the parking lot from the company's headquarters, concealed behind hedges. His office, however, would make any lawyer proud: it is large and wood-paneled, with original art on the walls and a commodity-price monitor on the credenza.

Diversification as practiced at Harris Farms is said to be the future for profitable agriculture, because it allows the clever manager to stay a step ahead of demand. Midwestern farmers have some ability to shift among the products their environment will support: wheat, corn, soybeans, sorghum, and livestock. For example, when grain prices fall and livestock prices rise, farmers can feed their grain to the stock and sell it ultimately as meat. Trends in the supply of these commodities tend to be parallel, however, and so the degree to which midwestern farmers can diversify often does not amount to much. Being able to shift among unrelated crops—cotton to onions to lettuce—makes for better protection against the erratic market. Working with small specialty crops also enables growers to get an idea of where they stand relative to the competition. Lobmeyer explained: "There are eleven million acres of cotton fields scattered all around the United States. Realistically, there's no way we can get a sense of what other cotton growers are doing. But there are just 294,000 acres of process tomatoes in the country, and 84 percent of them are here in California."

Harris Farms operates almost entirely without federal subsidies. Most of its crops aren't eligible for support. Harris does not enroll his cotton and wheat acreage with the CCC, because, he said, the maximum loan is inconsequential for a 17,000-acre enterprise and not worth the bother of going after.

Despite his computers, his economies of scale, and his lack of dependence on the government, Harris is pessimistic. He told me, "At this point farmers have become capable of producing a surplus of just about everything. The regulated programs get all the attention, because they involve federal deficits and family farms, but profit margins in specialty crops are becoming almost as bad." The market for grapes, once a glamour crop, is more depressed than the market for corn. Citrus fruits are about the only crop widely agreed to be profitable this year—profitable, that is, for growers who weren't hit by a series of frosts in Florida and

Texas that cut supply. Harris observed that if the country had not experienced a cycle of poor weather for crops in three of the past five years, which led to disappointing yields, surpluses would be even greater than they are, and prices lower.

The weather of late has been unusually severe in southern Iowa, where the gullied bottomland is in any case ill-suited to farming. In 1983 the rain was so relentless that farms were flooded with mud. Pat and Nancy Meade, who live in southern Iowa, lost twenty of the hundred calves born on their farm that year because they drowned in the mud. A high percentage of the hard-luck farm stories presented as typical on television and in news-magazines have southern-Iowa datelines.

To some extent a bad year can be offset by the generous tax treatment accorded to agriculture. For example, many types of farm buildings and fruit trees can be depreciated, and deductions can be taken for supplies that will not actually be used until the following year. Played properly, the game allows the payment of taxes to be postponed almost indefinitely.

Investors who buy into farms do not, as popular lore would have it, "profit from losing money": the best investment is always one that makes money. The situation of a "tax farmer" is roughly like this. Say that a doctor in the 50 percent tax bracket has $100 in marginal income. If he does nothing, the government takes $50 and he keeps $50. If he shelters the money in a farm generating a $100 deduction, his tax bill is reduced by $50. In both cases the doctor walks away with $50. But in the second case he also has some equity in the farm.

Since the doctor keeps $50 no matter what, all the investment has to do is make a dollar and he will come out ahead. Thus a commercial farmer who needs a decent income to care for his family is at a disadvantage with respect to a tax farmer for whom any income is pure gravy.

In the long run agriculture's favored tax status may do farm families more harm than good, because shelters encourage the overproduction that is at the core of agriculture's problems. From one pocket the government hands out tax breaks to encourage more farm investment and from the other it hands out subsidies to compensate for the depressed prices that investment causes. Nevertheless, farm-state legislators have extreme difficulty opposing any measure presented as a "farm tax break."

Surrounded by Surplus

Agricultural exports have stopped increasing over the past few years, after having grown steadily through the 1970s. The strength of the dollar is usually cited as the reason, and without doubt the strong dollar is a factor. But the growth trend in exports probably would have stalled regardless, because many countries are generating food surpluses of their own. Moreover, almost all of the industrialized countries have higher internal subsidies and more restrictive trade laws than we do.

In the late 1960s the countries in the European Economic Community met up to 90 percent of their demand for grain. In 1984, a bumper crop year, EEC farmers met 125 percent of that demand. U.S. agricultural sales to the USSR make headlines, but sales to Western Europe have been far more significant in volume. In 1983, for example, Europe bought about $10 billion worth of U.S. food—ten times as much as the Soviet Union did. Last year Soviet grain purchases hit a record high, and yet total sales to "centrally planned countries" accounted for just ten percent of U.S. exports. Asian nations are our best customers. In 1983 they bought $19.5 billion worth of U.S. agricultural products. But since then sales to Asia have been stable or falling.

World wheat production, 447 million metric tons in 1978, is expected to be 505 million metric tons this year   a 13 percent increase. Also since 1978 world rice production has increased by 20 percent and world cotton production by some 35 percent. In every part of the world except Africa and Japan food production is increasing faster than population.

The increased production, particularly in developing countries, can be attributed partly to the spread of modern technology and farming methods—progress that the United States has encouraged and in many cases has funded and supervised. We have a moral obligation to share our agricultural secrets with the world and should be proud that we have done so, but the cost has turned out to be greater than we expected. The world's increased production can also be attributed to U.S. farm-subsidy programs. For many commodities American support prices become the world floor prices, because whenever the going rate falls below what the CCC will pay, a significant portion of the supply is withdrawn from the market. Equilibrium between supply and demand is restored and the decline in the market price is halted. Nonrecourse loan programs, intended to limit the risk to American farmers, have the effect of limiting the risk to farmers in other countries, as well. For example, Argentina knew in 1981, courtesy of an act of Congress, approximately what the floor price for grain for the next four years would be, and thus could plan accordingly.

The agricultural programs of other countries are far more protectionist than those of the United States. Within the EEC agricultural commodities move freely, but what are in effect tariffs prevent food from being brought into the community at less than the regulated price. Thus American farmers are not permitted to undercut the market price in Europe, whereas any shipper may sell cheaply here. When the EEC has surplus grain, exporters receive direct subsidies to sell their overstock at below-market prices. The European subsidies are threatening to break the bank; several times in recent years the EEC Commission has recommended that the subsidies be cut, only to have farm interests in member nations beat the effort back. In 1986 Spain and Portugal—two potentially major agricultural producers—are expected to join the community, hide behind its tariff curtain, and use its subsidies to boost production.

Japan's regulations are even more stringent. Various restrictions limit the sale in Japan of U.S. commodities for which there might otherwise be higher demand—particularly beef and fruits. According to Yujiro Hayami and Masayoshi Honma, economists at Tokyo Metropolitan University, Switzerland has the world's most protectionist agricultural system, with domestic prices half again as high as the world average. Japan's is next, with domestic prices 45 percent higher than the world average. The EEC's domestic prices are 25 percent higher, and the United States, where domestic prices are slightly below the world average, ranks last in protectionism.

It is perhaps understandable that Europe and Japan, which have known famines in this century, should be anxious to keep farm production up. It's harder to understand the Reagan Administration's behavior. In March, President Reagan withdrew the pressure on the Japanese to observe voluntary auto-export quotas and asked nothing in return. If the Administration continues to push for cutbacks in U.S. agricultural production without insisting that members of the EEC cut back as well, subsidized European farmers will rush in to grab U.S. export markets.

We should be grateful that Japan has so little land, else it would surely make life as hard for American farmers as it has for American manufacturers. Another Asian country, however, has lots of land and a strong agricultural tradition: China. In 1980 China bought $2.3 billion worth of U.S. food and fiber. Now its purchases are down to $500 million and the country has begun to export cotton. Chinese officials have been stepping back from the commune system and introducing a limited form of capitalism in their fields; the results have been dramatic. Since 1978 China's cotton production has risen by 150 percent, its soybean production by 84 percent, its wheat production by 58 percent, and its rice production by 27 percent. Many production techniques used in China are backward (for example, cotton is shipped in nonstandard-sized bales, small enough for two men to lift manually), but Western methods and machines are being introduced. In China workers are accustomed to strict discipline and low wages; modern production could transform the country into the world's breadbasket. "They are much closer to it already than we like to think about," Kenneth Billings, the president of Fresno County's Federal Land Bank, says.

U.S. farm productivity by acre, which has declined slightly from its peak, in 1982, can be expected to rise again soon, as new hybrids, growth hormones, and chemicals come onto the market. A little further down the road gene splicing might make possible entirely new strains of plants that could spark another Green Revolution. The problems of oversupply in the future could make those today seem like warm-ups.

The Annual Crisis

Senate majority leader Robert Dole said recently that in every one of his twenty-five years in Congress there has been a farm problem. During the late 1940s President Harry S. Truman tried to cut back many farm subsidies and was rebuffed by a livid Democratic Congress. The Senate majority leader at that time, Scott Lucas, of Illinois, sounded very much like Dole when he complained of senators who "are constantly talking about economy in government . . . who have no hesitancy in getting off the economy bandwagon . . . to take care of their own communities . . . regardless of what the cost may be in the future." The Eisenhower Administration pushed through some farm-support cuts in

1953, but when it tried to go further, in 1958, it was defeated. That year Senator Allen Ellender, of Louisiana, argued, "This is not the time to lower prices farmers receive, particularly when farm income is already at an all-time low." New Deal descendant Lyndon Johnson moved to cut farm subsidies by $540 million in the budget he submitted in 1969, just before he left office. Nixon angered farmers with his attempts to change farm programs. Carter, a farmer, not only asked that subsidies be cut but stood fast during the 1979 tractorcade, refusing to make significant concessions.

The job of secretary of agriculture has chewed up most of those who have held it. Truman's "Brannan plan," named for Agriculture Secretary Charles Brannan, became a euphemism for political lunacy, the racetrack MX of its day. Radical farmers like some members of the American Agricultural Movement point to Eisenhower's Ezra Taft Benson as the first mastermind of the anti-farm conspiracy. LBJ's Orville Freeman, whose affiliation with the Minnesota Democratic Farmer Labor Party was beyond reproach, got into trouble by suggesting that cotton growers cut their prices in order to compete in the world market. Carter's secretary, Bob Bergland, who himself had been a farmer, ended his term amid acrimony. Now Reagan's secretary, John Block, formerly an Illinois hog farmer, is an object of scorn for having gone along with Reagan in the effort to cut farm subsidies. Block has hardly been helped by the fact that his former business partner, John Curry, was a plunger who bought up land with FmHA assistance and then defaulted. Every farmer I met in the Midwest knew about this case; some spoke of Curry as if he were a poisonous snake.

Partly because of the continuous anxiety to which they are subject, farmers have a long history of crying wolf. The agriculture committees, staffed by farm-bloc congressmen, do too. In 1965 a report of the House Agriculture Committee warned, "Hundreds of thousands of our most progressive farmers will find their debt positions intolerable and will be forced into bankruptcy"—language almost identical to that used last winter.

Checking old newspapers, I found that farmers have been proclaiming the "worst year since the Depression" regularly since the early 1950s. Reporting that placed the claim in historical perspective was rare, except for the occasional "down with farmers" piece that exaggerated in the other direction. Covering agriculture is a delicate matter for journalists, and especially for television crews. Someone who loses a farm loses his job, his home, and his way of life all on the same day. It would seem heartless of a reporter to mention that dispossessions are the exception or that thousands of other people experience tragedies that are of equal weight but that simply don't fit a news peg.

"They're taking away my land" is a plaintive cry of farmers, and when true, it's terrible to hear. Often it isn't true. A farmer who defaults on his loan is not losing his land so much as some part of his investment in it. The bank is the true owner of the farm, just as ultimately it is the owner of a mortgaged house.

Through the 1970s the farm bloc complained that farmers were being destroyed by inflation. Senator Jesse Helms, of North Carolina, who is the chairman of the Senate Agriculture Committee, said in 1981, "Farmers understand that unless this inflation is cured, they don't stand a chance." Now that the cure has taken effect, the *lack* of inflation is said to be a special hardship for farmers. Similarly, cries of "foul" were heard in response to the escalation in farmland prices while it was taking place, even though it was making holdings more valuable. Four years ago Catherine Lerza, the head of the National Family Farm Coalition, declared that high land prices had created a crisis for farmers. At about the same time Representative Berkley Bedell, of Iowa, proposed a $250 million Beginning Farmers Assistance Act to subsidize purchases of farmland. Now, of course, it is the decline in land prices that is said to pose a crisis for family farmers.

Using the Department of Agriculture's parity tables, some farm advocates claim that farmers are worse off today than ever. Parity tables are supposed to show the buying power of farmers; 1910-1914, when farm prices were strong, is taken as the base period and given a value of 100. In 1984 parity hovered around 59—that is, farmers had 58 percent of the buying power of their forerunners decades earlier. Figures like these are extremely misleading, however, because calculations of parity treat the present as if it were 1914. For example, they take into account the fact that tractors cost more but not that they do more. Parity makes an effective round of political ammunition, but it is not a reliable indicator on which to base policy. One farm-state congressional staff member told me, "Any farmer who seriously believes he would be living twice as well if it were 1914 again is crazy."

At a House Agriculture Subcommittee hearing in February, I gave up trying to count the number of times words like *desperate, disaster, unprecedented*, and *dying* were used. Representative Steve Gunderson, of Wisconsin, asserted, "Clearly, within the credit crisis confronting agriculture we are literally facing the fundamental destruction of rural society." Representative E. Thomas Coleman, of Missouri, declared that "farmers are faced with such high interest rates, declining land values, and low return for their products that they are reliving the Great Depression of the 1930s." At this hearing and throughout the battle over emergency aid, farm-bloc congressmen repeatedly predicted that as many as 10 percent of the nation's farmers could go bankrupt by March 1—the traditional deadline of banks for issuing spring planting loans—if substantially more than $650 million was not provided. A bonus-credit-aid bill was passed but Reagan vetoed it. The first of March came and went, the wave of foreclosures that was supposed to sweep the country did not occur, and the story vanished.

Resisting pressure for spending is a recurring challenge in Washington, and the ability of even conservative Republicans from farm country to forget their speeches about deficits and call for more agricultural subsidies has been remarkable for years. Farmers make powerful claims on the legislature in part because they make up a high percentage of the population in rural communities. In heartland congressional districts almost everyone is tied to the farm economy. No other constituent group—not auto workers in Detroit or gas producers in Louisiana—places such a statistical lock on its representatives.

Another running theme in Washington is the demand for a crackdown on rampant waste in somebody else's program. Farm groups are among those who have most vociferously protested the federal debt, which contributes to high interest rates and the strength of the dollar. But they also want more spending for farms, which would drive the deficit up. Last winter five of the country's largest agricultural associations formed a lobby called the Balanced Budget Brigade. While some spokesmen were making the rounds on Capitol Hill, demanding that the deficit be slashed, others were demanding extra credit aid. During his appearance on *Nightline* Governor Janklow sneered at Congress's failure to balance the budget—a feat that even New Right thinkers admit will be out of the question for many years—and boasted that states balance their budgets. Janklow didn't add that the main reason why state budgets are balanced is that federal grants supply 18.5 percent, on average, of state revenue. If a cosmic philanthropist made an 18.5 percent contribution to the federal budget, then the federal budget would also balance.

Finding solutions for a chronic problem like agricultural overproduction can vex democratic systems, which almost inevitably focus their attention on the demands of the moment. "Every time we do a farm bill, the short-term outlook—what happens one year down the road—overwhelms all other considerations," William Hoagland, the deputy staff director of the Senate Budget Committee, who was raised on an Indiana farm, told me recently. "In 1981 all we talked about was inflation, which turned out to be a moot point almost immediately after we finished debating it. This year it's debt. What we want from agriculture, what our long-term goals ought to be, stands no chance [of consideration], compared to whatever was in that morning's paper."

Eventually Congress will have to face the fact that there are too many farmers. The farm bill that Reagan has proposed, which in effect would abandon those parts of the federal program that subsidize the least successful farmers, may not be perfect, but so far it is the only one to concentrate on the problem of overproduction. The solutions to that problem do not lie solely in the realm of economic abstraction. They will involve a painful human cost. If the Reagan plan or something like it is enacted, Dennis and Patricia Eddy, for example, may lose their farm. That would not be a happy day for them or for any caring citizen. But the Eddys are young, responsible, bright, and eager to work. If they can't land on their feet, who can?

Early this year Representative E. Kika de la Garza, of Texas, the chairman of the House Agriculture Committee, said he might support changes in federal agriculture programs, but only if they could be achieved "without sacrificing one single farmer." This is like saying, Let's cut back that bloated defense budget—as long as no contractors lose work. There can still be family farms. It's just that not every person who wants a farm can have one, no matter how fervently we might wish he could.

PLOWED UNDER[2]

Beneath the surface, the tales of debt and displacement, the farm crisis has many elements, each a story unto itself. This one is about people still living on farms, people I met on a recent trip through four Middle Western states. What I learned from them—about the loss of history and tradition, the deterioration of trust between farmers and lenders, the profound poverty, and the broken human spirit it engenders—changed my thinking about the crisis.

Without Government assistance, farming today is a nonprofit activity. In the early 1980s, production burgeoned, prices fell, and interest rates soared. The same Farmers Home Administration (FmHA) that invited farmers to expand in the 1970s now worked overtime to get families off their farms. Despite farmers' repeated calls for a Government policy endorsing greater cost-price parity, the FmHA—originally set up to aid farmers—now acted more like a collection agency.

These abrupt shifts in the rules left farmers confused and hurt. They found themselves seeking new ways to deal with new realities: learning the law, organizing politically, taking up arms against authorities (and, in some cases, themselves). Their stories paint a stark portrait of a way of life betrayed.

Bill and Linda Lehman

Bill and Linda Lehman live and breed horses on an idyllic hilltop farm in Wisconsin. While managing a successful hog farm with his father, Bill was encouraged by the FmHA to find one for himself. Bureaucratic foot-dragging and foul-ups delayed Bill's moving in for five crucial months, preventing him from planting crops and building vitally needed facilities for the hogs. He was eventually forced to work in the frost and snow, hammering with two pairs of gloves on, to build his barn. Meanwhile, he continued his other duties at his father's farm.

[2]Reprint of an article by Steve Brodner, free-lance writer, from *The Progressive*, 51:35–40. My. '87. Copyright © 1987, The Progressive, Inc. Reprinted by permission from The Progressive, Madison, WI 53703.

Bill's financial plan was thrown off balance by the increased costs of building in the winter. Soon he couldn't afford grain for his hogs and had to take an extremely high-interest loan. That spring, with the new facility completed and the crop planted, hog prices collapsed. The Lehmans had nothing to fall back on but Linda's horses.

"We wanted to make the transition from hogs to horses," says Linda, "but we couldn't get any financial assistance whatsoever. [The FmHA] said that Bill had thirty days to come up with his complete debt of $17,500, plus an additional $15,000 [an unwarranted advance payment] before he could ask for a hay-planting loan."

Now, under the pressure of what Linda calls the roughest month of her life, the Lehmans plunged into a horse-selling marathon, just meeting the thirty-day deadline. Finally current with the FmHA, they were denied the new loan.

"In some situations," says Bill, "it's not the farmer's fault at all; it's the lender. It was my first borrowing in seven years. They couldn't understand particulars. I had no grain. [The FmHA] just looks at the spread sheet."

A top-rated manager, Bill was recognized in a memo by the FmHA's county supervisor: "If Bill Lehman can't make it, nobody can." Within a few months, the same official wrote, "I recommend liquidation at the earliest possible date. This operation is a joke."

"When times are good," says Bill, "the lender is your best friend. When times are tough, he can be your worst enemy." Through this period of conflict, Bill and Linda, with the help of farm mediators, have become articulate technical warriors in a battle against a formidable adversary. After a full year of being current in their loans, they saw their farm poised for liquidation.

"FmHA must be responding to a policy to get rid of the family farm," says Bill. "They'll get large corporate farms in. And when you get, say, Occidental Petroleum running the farms, then you'll get the dumb bunnies like us to be farm workers. But what they don't understand is that nobody will run it as well as the farmers do. It will just be nine-to-five jobs. The only farms that do well are owned by their employees, because they have vested interests. They'll work overtime to make sure something is done right. If you're punching a clock when a cow is calving, you may lose the calf *and* the cow . . . and who cares? Ninety-nine per cent of farmers work their butts off to be out on the farms. They like farming, being out with the animals, a good environment. Not to make a million dollars. To be able to turn on the lights, that's all we want. That's all we want. That's all we've ever wanted."

Jim and Fern Clausing

Having lost their farm, Jim and Fern Clausing of Carroll County, Missouri, are fighting for their home. The Farmers Home Administration wants it in the settlement of a large debt going back several years during which the Clausings, known as excellent managers, had some extremely bad luck.

First there was the contractor who sent a hog-breeding facility they were building into huge cost overruns. Then, for several months, their feed company delivered rotten grain, creating a state of gradual malnutrition in the hogs. Jim and Fern caught and vaccinated 250 baby pigs and saved a good number of them. But the balances and rhythms that a farm needs were lost now. The strain was great for the Clausings. Jim wound up in the hospital with the effects of chronic depression.

During this time the FmHA never sent them a notice for rescheduling and deferral of their loan, as is legally mandated. Neither did the agency advise them not to pay the feed company for the tainted product. In addition, it let the Clausings' application for a special debt set-aside program sit unprocessed for nine months. "We are overworked and understaffed. We have 260 cases," said county supervisor Kenneth Telgemeir at their appeals hearing. The hearing was held at the Carrollton FmHA office, where a sign calls farmers THE GREATEST PEOPLE ON EARTH.

The Clausings' former farm is now overgrown with weeds that obscure the weathered hog-farrowing houses. The fields are alive with grasshoppers.

"The main thing now is to keep the home," says Fern. "We can do it if we keep employed. In this area, employment is really bad. There's just no jobs. The farmland will eventually go to the FmHA and they'll probably let it go just like it's going now. A good part of the land that they've repossessed across the river is just weeds. It's not being used at all. I just don't think they know, in Washington, really what it's all about."

Wayne Brattrude

When Wayne Brattrude got out of the Army in the early 1970s, he decided to settle on his 130-year-old family farm in Wisconsin where he now lives with his father and sister. Needing financial help, he applied for a low-interest operating loan from the FmHA. While waiting for word, he resorted to private lenders. As interest rates skyrocketed in the early 1980s, the Brattrudes changed banks repeatedly in a search for affordable loans. Soon they were paying 17 percent interest to Thorp Finance.

"As soon as we got behind on the interest," says Wayne, "it went up to 21 percent. So we were paying 21 percent on $120,000. In six months, it was up to $130,000 and they were charging us interest on interest. So we ended up calling every Senator, Congressman, the Governor. We kept selling more hogs to pay off Thorpe's, till I was down to my breeding stock. If I'd sold *them* I'd be out of it. The Congressman, he'd call the FmHA office. The FmHA would tell him that I was ninth in line to get the loan. They'd just tell him stuff to pacify him. They told *me* that they didn't have the money.

"But we called Washington—it was an emergency; we were being foreclosed on—and a guy there said there was a fund, a slush fund, kind of, for this type of situation. I told him I've been trying to get a loan for years and years and now if we don't get it we'll lose the farm. So they sent a letter to Gunther [the FmHA county supervisor]. The letter sat in his office for three months. I confronted Gunther, but it got to the point where he wouldn't even answer the phone to talk to me.

"I finally got my FmHA loan. I got a 5 percent loan for forty years. But it was all through politics. I mean, it wasn't the fact of whether I was a good farmer or bad farmer, or whether I needed the money or didn't need the money. It was all politics. It was the pressure of people calling. And I had to get an FmHA-approved lawyer and give him a thousand dollars."

Roger Allison

Roger Allison is a farmer who devotes much of his time to helping other farmers. Running the Missouri Rural Crisis Center in Columbia, he works with those who are in trouble, advising them of legal options and accompanying them to appeals hearings.

His activism has personal origins. "In 1980, my Dad, who was an FmHA borrower, who had done everything the FmHA told him to do, had finished building a great big new hog-farrowing house and nursery," Roger says. "There were delinquent notes, and he needed more time to finish paying up. After it was built, they foreclosed on him. This devastated him. Farmers didn't know there was an appeals system through the Farmers Home Administration. When FmHA said, 'Get out,' you just got out. And if my Dad wasn't a strong-willed person, by God, he just might have. There were farmers all over our area being foreclosed on in 1980. And so we had our own little support group. And we retained a lawyer.

"In 1980, in the worst drought we ever had, my Dad was at the doctor's with my mother. And I was working on a combine—my farm adjoins his—and the cattle were bawling in the morning. A neighbor called and said, 'Roger, they're taking your Dad's cattle and machinery away!' So I called the attorney and he said, 'Okay, peacefully resist. They'll view this as a voluntary foreclosure if there's nobody there to say, "Hell no, don't take it!"'

"My Dad was in the appeals process [at the time]. The deputy sheriff was over there; he didn't have any court warrants. They didn't have anything. Well, I held them off a little bit and told them that my Dad was coming. That wasn't good enough. They were going to move those hogs anyhow. They had opened up this farrowing complex and nursery, that never had anybody in it except for the family, that used real sanitation procedures—boot cleaning, changing your clothes, not to spread disease. Here the doors were all open in the big, long building. Truckers were running through it, spreading disease and all kinds of crap, running the hogs around. They had the cattle up in a dry lot. It was 100 or some-odd degrees. I got into the loading chute and told them that I wasn't letting them move anything else out of here. So the deputy sheriff said, 'Well, Roger, you know that what you're doin' is just gonna cause trouble for yourself. It's an inevitable thing. So you might just as well step out of the way or else you're gonna be in serious trouble.'

"And so I said, 'Tom, you do your job, whatever you think that is. I'm doin' what I gotta do.' And so the county supervisor said to me, 'Anything you do against me or my assistant you're doin' against the United States of America.' I'd been in Vietnam. I was decorated a couple of times. Got the Purple Heart. But this guy, well, I sort of had a flashback, and I'm thinking, Jesus, here is this guy doing an illegal seizure representing the Government. Who the hell was I fighting for . . . and why?

"So that started activating me. In 1982, my Dad, finally, through the appeals process, went to Federal court. The court found the FmHA's actions 'arbitrary, capricious, and an abuse of discretion that was unwarranted by the facts.' Fifteen days later, I received a letter from the FmHA to come into the county office and bring my records with me. So I brought them in and six months later they foreclosed on *my* farm.

"I was reading an article one night that said that, due to the 1978 Agriculture Act, there's some people who think that FmHA borrowers have more due process. So I sent it to my lawyer and said, 'Check this out, maybe it could be helpful.' That formed the basis for the national class action suit [*Coleman v. Block*, 1983]. I was the first farmer that won, all the way to the Court of Appeals, a decision that the FmHA couldn't foreclose on a farmer until it offered, by due process, the opportunity to ask for a deferral of his interest and his loan principals. They couldn't foreclose until they wrote the rules and regulations. So they've written them now. So now I'm back in the appeals process."

Dennis and Lou Ann Scheuermann

Dennis and Lou Ann Scheuermann live in a trailer some fifty yards from a barn that looks ready to fall over. When Dennis moved his family and dairy herd to the Mondovi, Wisconsin, farm in 1971, he realized he had to make a decision.

"I could continue milking in the old barn till it couldn't be done anymore, build a new building, or get an off-the-farm job. I chose to build the barn," he says.

The bank wanted to help. Farmer and lender worked out a plan to replace the old barn with a new one, and also put up a facility for young calves, which they needed to retain a Grade A rating for their milk. With the first building complete, the economy quaked under the Scheuermanns. Dairy prices and land values began to decline, as did the bank's commitment to the plan for the second building.

Into the hard winter months, with only a wait-and-see message from the bank, Dennis and Lou Ann had to keep young calves in their only barn with the other cattle. Eventually this practice, viewed as unsanitary by the U.S. Department of Agriculture, caused their dairy herd to lose its Grade A rating. And that brought a significant loss of income for the farm. In ten years' time, the money for the young-stock facility never came.

"We've deteriorated quite a bit," says Dennis. "Meanwhile the old barn isn't usable. We're just treading water; going down every year. We're losing our equity. We have to borrow each year but we got no operating loan last spring. I put my crop in with a refund check from my taxes. I sold a couple of cows. Put in fewer acres of crops. Bought cheaper seed. I didn't use as much weed killer. Bought less fertilizer. I didn't use as much nitrogen for corn. And our crops show it now. So now we're negotiating with the Farmers Home Administration and the bank, which will probably foreclose on us."

"We've got the new barn," says Lou Ann, "but there's no place for the baby calves. You can't put them out in weather like this. We'd go to the loan officer, and all he'd say is, 'Just sit tight, just sit tight.' I'll hear those words as long as I'm here, and beyond maybe."

John Stevenson

John Stevenson and his family have lived their whole lives on farmland in Dane County, Wisconsin, settled by his great-great-grandfather in 1851. An expert cattleman, he once had 800 head in his herd. He now depends on his corn crop to fight off his debt. Having expanded his farmland in the 1970s from 280 to 440 acres, he got caught when grain prices and land values plummeted. What had seemed like a sound investment was now costing him dearly. He had to start selling cattle to pay his lenders. Because of his herd's diminishing numbers, he was denied renewal of his annual operating loan.

"The bank was charging me 21 percent interest on $200,000," says John. "You can't make up that kind of interest on a farm even if you *had* everything paid for. So I got the loan from the Federal Land Bank and paid the bank off. I rented part of the farm for three years to a guy who didn't pay me on time. The Federal Land Bank called and asked, 'Did John make his payments?' They started foreclosure action on me.

"This is what happens when you get in trouble. [Lenders] start calling around. One person finds out you're in trouble, then two, then everybody's right on you. The last three years, I've only taken one operating loan . . . and paid it back. This year I went to the bank and asked them if they'd put up twenty grand. They couldn't do that. So I went ahead and put the crop in myself. Now I owe the fertilizer company and I owe the seed company. But I'd done business with the fertilizer company since they've been there. And the seed-corn company my Grandpa did business with in 1910. Some people work with you and some work against you.

"There's been a lot of hard times here in 135 years and somebody's always stuck with it. If you *do* stick tough and things *do* turn around, that's the only chance you got of making back what you lost. It's gonna have to change. I'm not doing all this for nothing. I ask my son if he's gonna want to farm. He says, 'Dad, if I have to put up with what you had to put up with, why do it?'

"Last year, I slackened on a few things. I've spent more time on the phone trying to get financing than I did on the tractor. It kind of drains you right out."

AMERICA'S FARMERS: DESPERATE IN THE MIDWEST[3]

The place was St. Paul School of Theology in Kansas City, Missouri, the occasion the Second Annual Consultation on Town and Country Ministry, drawing some 75 United Methodist pastors, laypersons and judicatory executives from five midwestern states.

Although the schedule listed such topics as "Visioning Vital Mission in Town and Country Congregations" and "How to Organize a Cooperative Parish," for many of us the real subject needing to be discussed was the crisis in rural America. It made its way into the question-and-answer periods; it was referred to during morning worship; it kept an ad hoc group discussing issues and strategies long into the night; and it prompted the Nebraska delegation to draft a strongly worded letter to the United Methodist Council of Bishops calling for awareness and support from

[3]Reprint of an article by Judith L. Woodward, *The Christian Century*. Reprinted by permission from *The Christian Century*, 102:372. Ap. 17, '85. Copyright © 1985 by *The Christian Century*.

the church as a whole. Many of the conference participants took time to sign the statement as they hurried away from the last lecture.

In the late-night ad hoc group, people described several attempts at dealing with the problem. A farm crisis hot line has been set up by Interchurch Ministries of Nebraska, that state's organization for ecumenical cooperation. Funded by 14 denominations and one federal agency, the hot line provides a wealth of referral resources for those needing legal, financial or emotional help, as well as continuing contact with a field staff person who probably has experienced similar stresses. We were told that the hot line services are so desperately needed that it took one farmer eight hours to get through to the hot line number. A Missouri pastor told us that farm suicides in his state had tripled during the past two years, with most of the increase occurring in Missouri's relatively wealthy northern half.

An Iowa pastor who had taken part in recent farm rallies articulated the growing sentiment that government decisions made in the near future might determine whether the United States continues in the Jeffersonian pattern of family-owned farms or moves toward the South American pattern of landed gentry (or corporations) controlling most of the nation's agriculture. He stressed the need for interest buy-downs for family farms threatened by exorbitantly high annual interest rates.

Several days earlier, at an all-too-well-attended farm-crisis meeting in my own southern Nebraska county, I had heard the director of the Nebraska farm hot line say nearly the same things. Afterward I had listened to farmers talking about the speech. They had agreed that loan guarantees were a Band-Aid approach; what they really need are lower interest payments and higher prices for their crops, which they are currently selling for less than the cost of production.

Another pastor, experienced in university extension work, cautioned that there are no easy answers. "If we get the price of corn up, hog farmers will be in greater trouble," he told us. A judicatory executive who has worked with world-hunger needs concurred. "The problem needs to be looked at from a global perspective. It involves monetary policy and government budget deficits, among other things. Careful study needs to be done and hasty action should be avoided."

While the underlying issues are complex, a large part of the farm problem clearly has to do with current federal budget priorities and the mounting deficit that is helping to keep interest rates high and the dollar strong on world markets. President Reagan simultaneously vetoed legislation to aid farmers, saying that it was too costly, and asked Congress to approve the production of more MX missiles—which it did. Without greatly raising the federal deficit, these missiles can be funded only by implementing presidential proposals that would tear at the very fabric of life in the midwestern farm belt: eliminating the Small Business Administration (while small businesses are failing in every farming community); closing down the network of soil conservation offices (while futurists are warning that the loss of our topsoil may be the century's greatest disaster); and further cutting Medicare (while our local hospital, reeling from previous cuts, is struggling to stay open). The first thing that the MX will destroy is our country's agricultural heartland.

On Ash Wednesday, the church bells in many communities tolled for the plight of the American farmer. People outside our five-state area—church members, church leaders, legislators and government officials—need to hear and respond to the tolling of those bells before it is too late. If they do not do so, in the Midwest the small farm, the small town and the small church may become things of the past.

II. FARM COMMUNITIES UNDER STRESS

EDITOR'S INTRODUCTION

Recent films like *The River* and *Country* have dramatized the distress of farmers and their families at the threshold of foreclosure. This experience has been only too common in the 1980s, when almost a third of the nation's 630,000 full-time farmers are in danger of going under. The incidence of suicide in the farm belt has increased markedly, together with the breakup of marriages and other symptoms of deep frustration. In many cases, farms have been handed down from generation to generation, and their loss is felt by those affected as a virtual betrayal of their heritage, destroying their sense of identity. But farm failures also involve suffering in adjacent communities. In states like Iowa and Nebraska, where at least half of the jobs are tied to agriculture, it is sometimes said that "when you scratch a farmer, the rest of the community bleeds." Tractor and farm equipment sales suffer, local businesses are pinched, professional people move away, schools close, and small towns become all but deserted.

The first article in Section II, an editorial from *The Nation*, discusses the erosion of farm communities in South Dakota, the Corn Belt, and the High Plains—conditions for which politicians have no ready answers. A second piece from *The Nation*, by Osha Davidson, addresses the "rise of the rural ghetto" in the Midwest. As Davidson points out, not merely a "farm crisis" exists but a "rural community crisis" as well. As farmers fail, a loss of jobs occurs throughout the area, essential services are curtailed, and welfare immigrants move in from small towns to take advantage of cheaper housing. In an article from *U.S. News & World Report*, Michael Bosc points out the *human* cost of farm failures. Mental health facilities become overcrowded, farm "hotlines" are choked with calls, and aggressive violence against others soars. In a final piece, from the *New Republic*, Jeffrey L. Pasley concludes gloomily that families might be better off, under such conditions, to migrate to the cities.

BROKEN HEARTLAND[1]

It has been a harsh, bitter winter in the Corn Belt and the High Plains. Snows began early in October, and wind-chill factors of 50 degrees below zero have been common. A brief thaw may help, but everyone knows more crunching cold is ahead. More unsettling than the winter, which people on the prairies are used to, is the uneasiness related to the farm crisis.

Last month, in Union County, which has the richest land in South Dakota, a young Farmers Home Administration supervisor killed his wife, daughter, son and dog while they slept, then went down to his office and shot himself dead. He left a note: "The job has got pressure on my mind, pain on left side." The wife had been fired from two secretarial jobs in two years. The family was from New York State and had lived in three South Dakota towns in the past nine years. The 12-year-old daughter had written a poem in school expressing her pain at having to move so often and leave new friends behind. Because the father was an out-of-stater, the FmHA moved him about the state, apparently figuring he would be more willing to get tough with local farmers who were behind on their loan payments than would a native South Dakotan.

South Dakota farmers are accustomed to hard times. The old-timers remember "the thirties," when the drought came, the dust blew and they put up tumbleweed hay to try to keep their few remaining cattle alive. The price of corn was so low that the farmers burned the ears in their coal stoves. Now nightmares of those years haunt the people.

Over in Worthington, Minnesota, some 250 farmers gathered recently to hear an activist tell them that they "have no moral obligation to repay an unjust debt" and that they would be right to use a gun to defend their farms from foreclosure. Enough of the lawless spirit of the Old West remains in rural America for people to reach for guns when all else fails.

Community spirit in the hinterland of America is not dead, but it is eroding. People still contribute rather small amounts to

[1]Reprint of an article by Bob McBride, United Methodist minister in South Dakota. Reprinted by permission from *The Nation*, 242:132-3. F. 8, '86. Copyright © 1986 by *The Nation*.

food pantries to help the most needy. But as they see their neighbors go bankrupt and move away, many take the community-destroying attitude that "people get what they have coming to them." Farmers who "have it made" (that is, happened to be around during the good years), or those who have not yet realized that they too are in danger, say, "He went in too deep," or "He should have known better than to take out all those loans."

Small towns are hard hit. High schools are closing as young families move to the city; those who remain are reluctant to have children in these uncertain times. Rural and small-town churches are rapidly losing members and are largely supported by the elderly.

On Saturday evenings some people tune in to "A Prairie Home Companion," broadcast out of St. Paul over American Public Radio, and enjoy Garrison Keillor's apt description of life in Lake Wobegon, which seems so much like their hometowns. They know that there is something good about life in small-town America, but they wonder what is happening to that life in a high-tech, computerized, urbanized, war-threatening world. The only area of South Dakota that is booming is Ellsworth Air Force Base, near the Black Hills, to which cruise missiles and preparations for B-1 bombers have brought a fleeting prosperity.

The people are patriotic and for years have given their sons, and now their daughters, to the armed forces. Now they sense that the high-tech military binge is costing the nation a sound agriculture, and they ask, "Is this military overspend necessary?"

Congressional elections will be held this fall, and good candidates are surfacing in both parties. The incumbents, loaded with PAC money, claim that they have been the farmers' best friends in Washington, but they are in trouble as the distress in the Farm Belt grows more serious.

Meanwhile, the people of rural South Dakota, the Corn Belt and the High Plains, go valiantly ahead with life as usual as best they can. The high-school basketball games and tournaments are the main action in the towns fortunate enough still to have high schools. People still go to church, pray for the sick and troubled, try to help their neighbors when they can, and hope for a turnaround.

Unlike Garrison Keillor's Lake Wobegon, "where all the women are strong, all the men are good-looking, and all the children are above average," the people of small-town America feel they are going down the tube, and that neither the government nor anyone else in high-tech America gives a damn.

THE RISE OF THE RURAL GHETTO[2]

A blight that is economic rather than botanical is transforming small towns in the Midwest into rural ghettos—pockets of poverty, unemployment and despair. Although its spread is receiving little attention from the press and even less from politicians, it will be affecting people's lives there well into the next century.

The phrase "rural ghetto" is used by Michael Jacobsen, an assistant professor of social work at the University of Iowa. Jacobsen cautions against using the simplistic phrase "farm crisis" to characterize the region's problem. "It's not really a *farm* crisis at all," he says. "It's a rural community crisis." The forced liquidations played up in the media represent only one aspect of the general rural decline. The depressed agricultural economy is triggering a series of complex reactions that are devastating small towns.

The drop in farm income translates almost immediately into a drop in retail sales for local businesses. Predictably, businesses that sell mostly to farmers are having the worst time, but all are hurting. Retail sales in Iowa's rural communities have slipped an average of 25 percent in the past decade. The decline in sales caused by reduced farm income has, in turn, set off a record number of business failures throughout the state.

David Ostendorf, director of the rural advocacy group Prairiefire, has been watching the effects of the depressed farm economy on small communities for the past several years. "For every five to seven farms that go out of business, you can figure on one business in town folding," he says. "And when even one business closes in a small community it creates a ripple effect that's felt throughout town. Each job lost means there is that much less money circulating in the community, being spent at the super-

[2]Reprint of an article by Osha Davidson, Iowa-based journalist. Reprinted by permission from *The Nation*, 242: 820-21. Je. 14, '86. Copyright © 1986 by *The Nation*.

market, the hardware store or the barber shop. When sales drop at these other businesses, some are forced to close, and that means more lost jobs and less income to be spread around."

The closures sweep through a small town like a combine through a cornfield. As the local tax base erodes, schools are forced to consolidate, which destroys more jobs. This can be the deathblow for many small towns where the school is a major employer.

At that point, says Jacobsen, the transformation from small town to rural ghetto accelerates. "Anyone who can move out of town will go," he says. "There's nothing left there—no jobs, few stores and no community services to speak of. It's certainly no place for children, which is ironic because many of these people moved to small towns precisely because they seemed like good places to raise kids."

Not everyone is able to leave town, however. According to Jacobsen, most of those left behind fit into one of three main groups. First, there are the elderly, people who have lived in the area all their lives and who are unable physically, economically and emotionally to leave. Many of them are retired farmers and most are living on Social Security benefits. The only equity they have is in their homes, for which there is no market.

Elderly people in decaying towns face a variety of problems, including the inaccessibility of health care. By the time a town reaches the final stages of disintegration, most doctors, nurses and pharmacists have moved on to more prosperous communities. Many old people find it difficult to drive twenty or thirty miles to the closest doctor or pharmacist. For the poorest of them, it is impossible.

The second group populating the new rural ghetto consists of unemployed or underemployed young people. Most of them never attended college; many dropped out in high school. They are now stuck in a town with no industry and few businesses.

"Some people think that these kids will simply move down to the Sun Belt and find work," says Jacobsen. "But that's just not happening. When you've lived all your life in a small Midwestern town you're not apt to pick up and move to an industrial center in a different part of the country. And there are a limited number of jobs in the Sun Belt anyway."

The third group is the welfare immigrants. Jacobsen says these people are playing an increasingly important role in the transformation of small towns.

"We're seeing an influx of people from larger cities who are dependent on public assistance and who are moving to small towns to take advantage of cheaper housing there," he says. "Moving from a larger city can seem to be a very attractive alternative to a single mother on Aid to Families with Dependent Children. She can rent an entire house for $100 to $150, compared with the $300 or more she was paying for a small apartment in the city. The problem is that once she moves from Dubuque to North Branch, she's trapped there, with no hope of finding work and getting off welfare."

Because the word "ghetto" has traditionally referred to an urban phenomenon, it may be hard for many people to take Jacobsen's warnings seriously. But there is ample evidence that the sorts of problems found in city ghettos—poverty and malnutrition, unemployment and chronic dependence on welfare, a sense of desperation and a resultant rise in the level of violence—are now becoming common in their rural counterparts.

Last year the number of farm families in Iowa receiving food stamps soared by 400 percent. Social workers say that cases involving spouse and child abuse are on the upswing, and Iowa Youth and Shelter Services reports a sharp rise in the number of rural runaways.

Joanne Dvorak, a mental health professional with the Family Services Agency in eastern Iowa, has seen an increase in violent incidents among rural families as they struggle to survive. She has also observed with alarm the increase in suicides in the area, as some people simply give up the fight. "A lot of people, on the farm and in town, are pretty distressed," she says. "And you can't blame them; they're watching their communities and their lives disintegrate around them."

According to a study by Larry Swanson, an economist and the former director of the Great Plains Office of Policy Studies at the University of Nebraska, all rural Nebraska communities with a current population of under 1,000 will be barely surviving by the 1990s if Federal policy stays on its present course. Swanson and other experts say that any long-term solution must include two components: a Federal program that effectively manages farm production, ending the chronic overproduction that leads to reduced farm income; and a revision of the U.S. tax code, terminating agriculture's status as a tax-sheltered industry.

Don Ralston, co-director of the Nebraska-based Center for Rural Affairs, agrees that the tax code encourages farm expansion and benefits large farms at the expense of small and middle-sized ones. Ralston points out that a large number of small and middle-sized farms are necessary to the health of Midwestern rural communities. The viability of business in small towns depends on the number of people living and buying in the area, not on the number of acres farmed. As one agriculture researcher put it, "One person only needs one haircut."

Little is being done at the state level to help small communities. "Sometimes I honestly think that the state government in Iowa has written off small towns," says Jacobsen. "Nobody says that outright, but when you read the proposals coming out of the State Legislature, you can see that they're just not dealing with what's happening."

As politicians profess a deep and abiding love for "heartland values," thousands of small towns spread out across the Midwestern countryside are left to wither on the vine.

FAMILY LIFE TAKES BEATING IN FARM CRISIS[3]

Jim King has seen father turn against son. He has seen marriages fall apart and once responsible men become alcoholics. But King says it could be worse: At least, this depressed farming community of 2,200 in western Illinois has seen no suicides. Yet.

What Cambridge is witnessing is being repeated across the farm belt as an economic crisis "rips the social fabric of rural America," says King, who runs the Spoon River Community Mental Health Center.

Grim statistics show that one-third of the nation's 675,000 family-size commercial farms are in serious financial trouble and that some 43,000 farms went under during the first half of 1985. The Farm Credit Administration is carrying more than 11 billion dollars in bad loans. Iowa has lost more than 5,000 Main Street firms in three years.

[3]Reprint of an article by Michael Bosc, *U.S. News & World Report* staff writer. Reprinted by permission from *U.S. News & World Report*, 99:62. N. 18, '85. Copyright © 1985 by *U.S. News & World Report*.

Numbers on the social costs of the agricultural depression are just as distressing. Missouri reports 71 farm suicides last year—up 160 percent from 1983. The Southwest Iowa Regional Mental Health Center is counseling 69 percent more clients than in 1980—most of them farmers under stress.

Sense of loss. In a study of Missouri families forced off their farms, 74 percent of the men reported that the foreclosure made them feel worthless, 49 percent said they had become more physically aggressive and 10 percent admitted to continued alcohol abuse.

These woes pile up in rural America because "losing a family farm is a lot like losing a family member," says Dean Oswald, county agent for Henry County, where Cambridge is located.

For the moment, the bountiful fall harvest is lifting the spirits of farmers some. But that's only temporary. "Whatever money they make is all going to the banker," says William Heffernan, a University of Missouri rural sociologist. "Meantime, the stage is set for some extreme things to happen."

Experts assert that the rural suicide rate already is understated and that the deaths often are staged as farm accidents so families can collect insurance. "Local coroners and medical examiners don't want to stigmatize the family, so if there's the slightest doubt, they call it an accident," notes Paul Lasley, an Iowa State University sociologist.

Increasingly, farmers make no effort to conceal their distress. In Clay Center, Kans., this summer, one farmer stuck the muzzle of a shotgun into his mouth and held it there for three quarters of an hour before a deputy sheriff yanked it away.

Equally alarming is the potential for aggressive violence against others. "I have heard talk of burning the crops or burning the bank," says Joan Blundall of the Northwest Iowa Regional Mental Health Center. Nye Bouslog, a farm financial counselor for the Illinois Extension Service, knows of one farmer who destroyed his machinery rather that let the banks repossess it.

Behind such actions is a tendency of a down-and-out grower to blame someone else for his problems, such as a banker for lending him too much money or the government for encouraging him to overproduce.

Hate groups are finding fertile ground in rural areas, and anti-Semitism in particular is mounting. Law-enforcement authorities in Kansas, Nebraska and Iowa reported increased activity last summer by militant right-wing outfits such as Posse Comitatus, the Aryan Nations and the Covenant. They find converts, says Tam Ormiston, head of the farm division of the Iowa Department of Justice, "for the single reason that more and more farmers are finding traditional approaches to be ineffective in resolving their problems."

Alarmed Jewish leaders held meetings in October in Des Moines, Kansas City, Iowa City and Sioux City to discuss how to deal with what Daniel Goldstein, executive director of Kansas City's Jewish Community Relations Bureau, calls "the most serious threat to American Jewry I can recall."

Trouble calls. How to cope with the spreading agriculture crisis and blunt its antisocial consequences is becoming the No. 1 priority of social agencies.

Churches and rural organizations are sponsoring support groups and crisis centers. The farm hot line in Walthill, Nebr., received 1,050 first-time calls in its first year of operation. "It's desperation time," says operator Judy Dye. Last year, callers asked: "How do I refinance?" This year, the question is: "I lost my farm—what do I do?"

Pete Brent of Prairiefire, a farm-activist group based in Des Moines, says hot-line operators are being trained to handle suicide threats. "When they say things like, 'The silo looks real attractive' or 'The shotgun's out in the pickup,' we try to keep them talking." One basic rule: The more detailed the suicide plan, the more serious the threat.

Many rural ministers have turned to psychologists and mental-health counselors for advice, and a number of churches have begun support groups. Says the Rev. Dave Shogren of Sibley, Iowa, "The support group is a forum for them to get it all out— the anger, the frustration. There, people can really spill their guts."

Shogren runs a separate support session for rural merchants. "A lot of these small businessmen are in the same position the farmers were a year ago—loans are being called in, and the banks are saying let's check this out again," he observes.

But support groups and hot lines are only, in the words of one rural social worker, "a safety valve, a Band-Aid." The real medicine for the social misery in the nation's heartland is genuine improvement in the farm economy.

"What we have is a chronic problem with no immediate solution," says Blundall of the Northwest Iowa center. "And no one's saying this situation is going to improve in four or five years."

THE IDIOCY OF RURAL LIFE[4]

The bourgeoisie has subjected the country to the rule of the towns. It has created enormous cities, has greatly increased the urban population as compared with the rural, and has thus rescued a considerable part of the population from the idiocy of rural life.
> —Marx and Engels, *The Manifesto of the Communist Party*

If we let Republican farm policies drive our family farmers off the land, then your food won't be grown by farmers whose names are Jones or Smith or Anderson. No, your food will be raised by Tenneco Corporation, or Chevron, or ITT.
> —Senator Tom Harkin, Democrat of Iowa

The idea that people still farm for a living in 1986 is an alien and yet somehow romantic one, redolent of grandparents and "Little House on the Prairie." A 1986 *New York Times* poll reported that 58 percent of Americans believe that "farm life is more honest and moral than elsewhere," and 67 percent think that "farmers have closer ties to their families than elsewhere." Images of rural life dominate the "Americana" that passes for tradition in the United States. At a holiday like Thanksgiving, when we are supposed to give thanks to our Pilgrim ancestors and the "bounty" before us, we pay homage to the values embodied in the idea of the "family farm."

At one time, this reverence for farm life made sense. The United States began as an agricultural nation. In 1790, 93 percent of the American population worked on farms. Agricultural products made up 80 percent of exports. The Founders, knowing which side their breadbasket was buttered on, heaped extravagant praise on the nation's farmers. "Cultivators of the earth are the most valuable citizens," wrote Thomas Jefferson. "They are the most vigorous, the most independent, the most virtuous, &

[4]Reprint of an article by Jeffrey L. Pasley, *New Republic.* Reprinted by permission from the *New Republic,* 195: 24–7. D. 8, '86. Copyright © 1986 by the *New Republic.*

they are tied to the country & wedded to its liberty and interests by the most lasting bonds."

The "family farm" remained a powerful myth long after it ceased to be a political fact. "The great cities rest upon our broad and fertile prairies. Burn down your cities and leave our farms, and your cities will spring up again as if by magic; but destroy our farms and the grass will grow in the streets of every city in the country," thundered Populist leader William Jennings Bryan. Yet as the myth gained strength, Americans were actually leaving the farm by the millions. Though the number of farmers continued to grow until 1920, the cities grew much faster, and the percentage of the American population working in agriculture declined with every census after 1790. The figure dropped to 30 percent by 1910, and to three percent in 1985. As the country grew, it exposed its citizens to creature comforts and other opportunities to prosper more easily, which made it hard to keep the farmers down on the farm. As farmers sold out or quit, those who remained bought up their land. Average farm size increased from 152 acres in 1930 to 441 acres in 1985.

I grew up outside Topeka, Kansas, attended a rural high school that had an Ag-Science building but no auditorium, and graduated from a college in the Minnesota farm country. In my experience, the standard image of the farmer has more to do with urban romanticism than with reality. Yet when the most recent farm crisis hit the nation's front pages and movie screens in 1985, the "family farm" captured the national imagination. Journalists suddenly found the stuff of Greek tragedy in Ames, Iowa. "Beauty is a cruel mask," wrote Paul Hendrickson of the *Washington Post*, "when the earth rolls right up to the edge of the interstate, freshly turned. When the rosebud trees are bleeding into pinks and magentas. When the evening rain is soft as lanolin." And so on.

With the papers full of stories about farmers going out of business, committing suicide, or shooting their bankers, farm-state politicians and activists began to campaign for a program specifically to help "family" farms, a proposal that evolved into the "Save the Family Farm Act." Introduced in October by Harkin and Representative Richard Gephardt of Missouri, the bill would impose mandatory controls on the amount farmers could produce and the extent of land they could farm, and would force larger farmers to set aside a larger percentage of their acreage. The bill would roughly double commodity prices (followed by additional yearly increases), sharply increasing the cost of raw food products. A small price to pay, its proponents say, so that family farmers can afford to maintain their traditional way of life. For supporters of the bill, the question is not primarily economic. On humanitarian grounds, they want to preserve the family farm as a way of life. On social grounds, they want a Jeffersonian countryside of small, independent landowners. Yet when I asked Charles O. Frazier of the National Farmers Organization, which supports the Harkin bill, whether the measure might hurt farmers in the long run, he replied, "To hell with the long run, we're talking about running a business."

Farmers are just like everyone else. They want to make money and live better than their parents did—and better than their neighbors, if possible. Urbanites often confuse the folksy ways of some farmers with an indifference to material wealth and the refinements that it brings. The difference between farmers and city-dwellers lies not in a different attitude toward money, but in different choices about what to spend it on. Washington lawyers want to make money to buy a BMW and a vacation in Paris. The average farmer may prefer a big pick-up truck with floodlights on top and a motor home he can take to Florida for the winter. Indeed, the young farmers who are in the most trouble today got that way by expanding their operations too quickly in the 1970s. Farmers aren't uniquely greedy, just ambitious like any other businesspeople.

In any case, family ownership of farms is not in danger. Nonfamily corporations operate only 0.3 percent of the nation's farms, own only 1.6 percent of the farmland, and account for only 6.5 percent of total sales of farm products. Agriculture simply doesn't offer a big enough return to attract many large corporations. Though farmland has become concentrated in the hands of fewer landowners, more than half of the large farms are owned by families, in many cases organized as partnerships or family corporations. "The family farm today is grandpa, two sons, and some grandsons who all help manage the place. The family farm of the future is a family farm corporation. These are stronger operations than the old-style family farms," said Jim Diggins, vice president of Farmer's National Company, an Omaha farm management firm.

The USDA divides farms into five classes: rural residences ("hobby farmers"), small family, family, large family, and very large farms. The farm crisis has left the large and very large family farms relatively untouched. Because of their economies of scale, even when prices drop they can still make a profit. Large family farmers operate an average of 1,807 acres, hold an average of $1.6 million in assets, and clear an average income of around $78,000 a year; and they are located in areas where living costs are low. Families on very large farms hold an average of 3,727 acres and net an average annual family income in 1983 of almost $600,000.

What the Pa Ingalls fans have in mind are rural residences and small family farms, which usually occupy 300 acres or less. Although these small farmers make up two-thirds of the total, however, they do not depend on agriculture for their living. According to the USDA, their "off-farm income" has exceeded their "on-farm income" ever since 1967. The yeomen of 1986 till the soil only as a sideline, and make 90 percent to 100 percent of their income from jobs or businesses off the farm. So the "farm crisis" isn't impoverishing them.

In fact, just about the only ones really endangered by the current crisis are medium-sized family farmers. It is this group, which amounts to one-fourth of all farmers, whom the Save the Family Farm Act proposes to save. They are hardly what Jefferson had in mind. On average, they own about 800 acres with assets approaching $1 million. Despite their size, they are far from self-sufficient. These are the farmers, by and large, who depend on government subsidies. Their troubles lie in the basic economic facts of the institution. Unlike small farmers, who have other sources of income, or large farmers, who have diversified multimillion-dollar operations, the family farmer gets paid only when he sells his crops. In between harvests, he must borrow money if he is to stay in business and feed his family. In no other industry does a worker need to take out loans in order to keep his job. The farmer is at the mercy of the interest rate, as well as the weather and the grain markets. They have the vulnerabilities of workers and businessmen with few of the benefits—neither employment security and benefits on the one hand, nor freedom and the possibility of lavish income on the other.

These family farmers occupy a precarious center between the larger and smaller operations. Their farms are big enough to re-

quire full-time work but not big enough to lower costs or allow
them to take full advantage of new technology. In order to compete with the large farms, the family farmer has to invest in the
same expensive machinery and chemicals. Because he has fewer
assets, his debts are proportionately much higher. He often has
to sell his crop when he needs to make a payment, rather than
when the price is highest. His high costs relative to his size make
his profit margin razor-thin when it exists at all.

Thus medium-sized family farmers rely heavily on the increasing value of their land to help them pay their debts and get
new loans. While inflation plagued the rest of the country in the
1970s, family farmers experienced a boom, as food prices and especially land values climbed to unprecedented heights. When inflation slowed down in the 1980s, so did the farm economy,
sending land values through the floor. The farmers who invested
heavily in new land on the wave of rising values found themselves
hopelessly trapped when the values fell. The moral of this tale
cannot be missed: those family farmers' fortunes depended not
on their farming abilities, but on land values, a factor out of their
control. Their ownership of land made them only more dependent. According to the USDA, farmers that leased more land
weathered the crisis better, since they had fewer debts to pay at
inflated interest rates. The family farmer has always walked this
economic treadmill. The United States had its first farm crisis,
Shays's Rebellion in 1786, before it had a Constitution.

How, then, did American family farmers become, in Harkin's
words, "the most efficient and productive in the world"? Family
farmers can keep labor costs very low because the family provides
the bulk of the labor. Family farms operate under vastly different
labor standards than the rest of American industry. "Child labor
laws do not apply to family farms because family farms must have
child labor to survive," wrote Minnesota politician and family
farm alumnus Darrell McKigney. "Twenty or thirty years ago
farm families commonly had ten or more children. [With
automation] today five or six is a more common size." From a very
early age, family farm children participate in every phase of the
operation, from work with dangerous heavy equipment to close
contact with carcinogenic chemicals and disease-carrying animals. In numerous farm areas, so many children are taken out of
school at harvest time that the schools officially close until the

harvest is finished. Practices that would be outrageous at a textile mill suddenly become all warm and cuddly when they appear on the family farm.

Family farmers also achieve efficiency through a draconian work schedule that no self-respecting union would allow. "The farm family does physically demanding and highly stressful work at least 14 hours a day (often at least 18 hours a day during harvest season), seven days a week, 365 days a year without a scheduled vacation or weekends off," wrote McKigney. "The farmer must endure all of this without the benefit of a health plan, safety regulations, a retirement plan, workmen's compensation, or any of the benefits that most U.S. labor unions demand." Psychologist Peter Keller, past president of the Association for Rural Mental Health, pointed out that many farmers are permanently tied to their farms. A dairy farmer, for instance, cannot just take off for a two-week vacation and not milk his cows. "Farmers lose perspective on the other things in life," said Keller. "The farm literally consumes them."

And the family farm physically consumes those who work on it, too. According to the National Safety Council, farming is the nation's most dangerous job—more dangerous even than working in a mine. In 1983 farming clocked in at 55 job-related deaths per 100,000 workers, or five times the rate for all major industries combined. In 1984 Tom Knudson of the *Des Moines Register* published a Pulitzer Prize–winning series that cataloged the myriad health and safety risks run by farmers. Farmers working with powerful farm machinery face death or maiming by crushing, chopping, asphyxiation, or electrocution. ("As he reached for a stalk of corn dangling from the corn picker, Vern Tigges of Dexter felt a jolt. In the next moments in a fierce and frantic struggle with the machine, three fingers were ripped from his hand.") They may be poisoned by the nitrogen dioxide gas that accumulates in grain silos, or have their lungs permanently damaged from breathing the air in enclosed hog pens. They may be crippled by "farmer's lung disease," caused by moldy grain dust. They may develop leukemia from contact with herbicides used on corn. (Iowa farmers contract leukemia 24 percent more frequently than the average American.) Knudson wrote that recent health findings exploded "the myth of farming as the good life of fresh air and sunshine."

But what about the benefits of good-old-fashioned-lemonade values and the supportive friendliness of a rural community? Though hard data is difficult to come by, many small towns appear to suffer from teenage pregnancy, alcoholism, and other social maladies at rates that are higher than average. One New England study showed relatively high suicide rates among farmers during a period antedating the farm crisis. And rural communities haven't always stood by their financially troubled members. Sociologist Paul Lasley's Iowa Farm and Rural Life Poll reported that a majority of Iowa farmers felt they received little or no support from their churches, neighbors, schools, or local voluntary organizations. At a "town meeting" with Representative Tim Penny, Democrat of Minnesota, in New Market, Minnesota, I heard farmers ridicule the idea of slightly higher property taxes to improve the area's meager school system practically in the same breath that they demanded higher subsidies for themselves. These things never happened on "The Waltons."

The usual lesson gleaned from the facts of farm life is that there is nothing wrong with the family farm that higher commodity prices won't solve. Yet farm programs have come and farm programs have gone, and still farmers (and especially farmers' children) have left, for the simple reason that life is usually better off the farm. "It is a way of life, but so was the village blacksmith," says economist William H. Peterson. The urban "wage-slave" worker, for all his lack of "independence" and supposed alienation from his work, has some decided advantages over the rural yeoman. He has the security of a regular income, and definite hours set aside for his leisure. More often than not, the law guarantees the non-farmer a safe place to work, and protects him from the whims of his employer. The urban wage-earner has daily contact with a wide variety of other people, and access to cultural events and decent public services.

Proponents of Harkin-Gephardt and similar measures worry about where farmers will go once they leave the land. Yet former farmers do not just fade away. They have skills and work habits that many employers find attractive. (If they sell their farms, they will also have several hundred thousand dollars.) Growing farm management companies hire experienced farmers to manage large rented operations, under much more favorable terms and conditions than they could get on their own. Farmers working for others would demand better working conditions. Many states now have retraining programs for those who give up farming and want to learn a new trade or profession.

I saw the movie *Country* on a rainy Monday night in Topeka. Two farmers and their wives and a group of teenage girls were the only other people in the theater. The farmers complained loudly throughout the first hour of the film, and then left, shaking their heads in disgust. The girls sat through the final credits, sniffling at the plight of Sam Shepard and Jessica Lange. At a farm protest rally in Minnesota, I heard a song that went like this:

> Now some folks say
> There ain't no hell
> But they don't farm
> So they can't tell.

We should take the singer at this word. Tyrants from Stalin to Mao to Pol Pot have subjugated their populations by forcing them to "stay on the land." Given the conditions of life on the family farm, if ITT or Chevron or Tenneco really does try to force some family farmers off their land, they might well be doing them a favor.

III. EXPLAINING THE FARM CRISIS

EDITOR'S INTRODUCTION

In the present farm crisis, family farmers have suffered disproportionately, and many analysts regard the family farm's decline as part of an irreversible process that has been going on for decades. The family farm operates on a small profit margin, and when reverses in the economy occur has little room to negotiate its survival. It has, in fact, been kept viable only through government intervention. Some agricultural specialists, however, believe that the government has never constructed a truly effective program for the maintenance of the smaller farmer, since subsidies have tended to favor the big producers. At issue in the farm crisis, too, is the Green Revolution, the development of biotechnology that has revolutionized farming and created overproduction. Those best able to make use of the new technology are the superfarms, owned by consortiums, giant insurance companies, and large corporate investors, and managed by trained management experts. Less able to make use of the Green Revolution's advantages without incurring debt that in depressed times cannot be repaid, the smaller farmer has been confronted by foreclosures and stigmatized as a "bad manager."

In Section III of this compilation, a variety of writers comment on these developments. Heather Ball and Leland Beatty, in an article from *The Nation,* note that the total amount of interest payments on farm loans now surpasses the total net farm income, creating an untenable situation for the family farmer. As they view it, the smaller farmers are being squeezed out of agriculture by the superfarms which, by 1995, will produce 75 percent of all farm products. In the following article, reprinted from *The American Scholar,* William Mueller argues that the U.S. Department of Agriculture has traditionally favored "agribusiness" over family farmers, and devised a patchwork of programs designed to assist the smaller farmer but often working to his disadvantage. In one of many illustrations, he points to the Dairy Reduction Program of the 1985 Farm Bill, which offers incentives to small dairy farmers to sell their herds, while big dairy operations are permitted to expand. Writing in *The Public Interest,* three professors of agriculture (Elmer W. Learn, Philip L. Martin, and Alex F. McCalla) review U.S. farm subsidy programs from the Depression to the present, concluding that no consensus has existed as to whether there should be more or less government intervention. A final article, reprinted from *Science* magazine, is informative about global food production, the loss of overseas markets, and the emergence of expanded farm economies in countries ranging from the European community to Argentina and China.

BLOWING AWAY THE FAMILY FARMER[1]

The specter of foreclosure is haunting America's independent family farmers. That staple scene of nineteenth-century melodrama—the villainous banker demanding the mortgage payment on the old homestead—was revived in modern dress in the recent movie *Country,* with a bland bureaucrat from the Federal Farmer's Home Administration replacing the miserly Banker Jones. The forces threatening the thousands of real-life counterparts of Gil and Jewell Ivy, the couple facing eviction in *Country,* are more abstract and impersonal than the film suggests. The villains are policies of the Federal government that encouraged people like the Ivys to go into debt and then made it impossible for them to pay off that debt.

According to Emanuel Melichar, senior economist at the Federal Reserve Board, more than one-third of America's commercial farmers are in serious financial trouble, and unless real interest rates come down and debts are rescheduled, many of them will go under. An American Bankers Association survey conducted in 1983 found that 17 percent of farmers with outstanding loans would be unable to make their payments this year. For the first time in history, the total amount of interest payments on farm loans has surpassed the total net farm income. Under Reagan, real interest rates—the average rate minus the rate of inflation—have been the highest in the century.

[1]Reprint of an article by Heather Ball, a policy economist, and Leland Beatty, a policy analyst, for the Texas Department of Agriculture. Reprinted by permission from *The Nation,* 239:442–4. N. 3, '84. Copyright © 1984 by *The Nation.*

The debt crisis has fallen most heavily on middle-level farmers, those with gross annual sales of between $40,000 and $500,000. During the 1970s, the number of operators in this category increased by 250 percent. Some of the increase was due to inflation, which raised prices dramatically, but its primary cause was the Federal government's efforts to encourage production for overseas markets. In 1973, Washington sought to counteract ballooning U.S. trade deficits caused by the Organization of Petroleum Exporting Countries' oil embargo by expanding agricultural sales abroad.

Generous subsidies to overseas purchasers through loans from the Commodity Credit Corporation, an undervalued dollar and broad extension of credit to foreign governments by large commercial banks spurred a leap in U.S. farm exports from $8 billion in 1971 to $43.8 billion in 1981. Major purchasers included Poland, Argentina, Mexico and Brazil; all four bought grain on easy credit terms. In the 1980s these monetary and fiscal policies were suddenly reversed, as the international financial community realized debtor nations could not possibly repay their loans without severely cutting back on imports. The International Monetary Fund imposed austerity programs that turned off the tap on money to buy U.S. farm commodities.

In addition, an overvalued dollar due to high U.S. interest rates imposed a 32 percent surcharge on all U.S. exports, according to the 1984 "Economic Report of the President." As a result, agricultural exports dropped more than 20 percent between 1981 and 1983, and real prices on major commodities dropped 21 percent.

The family farmer is bearing the cost of the new policies in the form of low prices, high interest rates and plummeting land values. There has also been a dramatic shift in the structure of farming. "Superfarms," those with annual sales of more than $500,000, account for 25 percent of the total farm output in America, even though they constitute only 1 percent of all agricultural units. According to the Farm Credit System (F.C.S.), if the trend continues, superfarms will make up 6 percent of all farm units by 1995 and will produce more than 75 percent of all farm products.

F.C.S. studies make clear that net farm income will never reach the level of any year in the 1970s. The Department of Agriculture forecasts steadily declining crop prices through the decade.

Unless this direction is reversed, medium-sized operators will be squeezed out of business "like toothpaste out of a tube," as a leading agricultural economist put it. They will be replaced by large spreads owned by wealthy investors looking for tax shelters, or by high-equity farmers who want to expand their holdings.

If agriculture were an industry that had resisted innovation and showed declining productivity, perhaps an argument could be made for allowing uncontrolled market forces to clear out the deadwood. But America's decentralized, commercial family farm system is the most successful in the world. Farmers utilize the latest technology, lead the nation in productivity gains and maintain a global competitive advantage, despite the punishing effects of an overvalued dollar.

There is more at stake than economic efficiency, though. A recent study of Nebraska farmers by Larry Swanson, an economist at the University of Nebraska, concluded that if family farms continue to fail at the present rate, rural communities will deteriorate. Agriculture and family farmers in particular are the lifeblood of rural communities. They patronize local stores, have their equipment serviced at local shops and send their children to local schools. If the trend continues toward fewer, larger farms producing an increasing share of our food and fiber—and claiming an even larger share of farm income—school enrollments will decline by 15 percent, one out of every ten retail stores will close and the labor force will shrink by 7 percent before the decade is out. Many small towns will disappear.

The financial cost of widespread farm failures could be enormous: as much as $100 billion in uncollected loans and business losses. Not only will indebted commercial farmers go under, so will the rural businesses that depend on them. Agricultural banks have already quadrupled their standard loan loss rate (a measure of the reserves they maintain in anticipation of bad debts).

The present policies also encourage wasteful farming practices that do irreparable harm to the soil. Farmers burdened by debts cannot afford to take advantage of tax credits or low-interest loans for soil and water conservation. They have to plant fencerow to fencerow in a desperate effort not to fall further behind in their payments. Unless their debt problems are addressed, they cannot practice careful stewardship of the land.

A new Federal farm policy is needed to undo some of the damage caused by the government's massive shift in direction

over the past decade, without bringing back the ruinous overpro-
duction-at-any-cost policy of the early 1970s. A long-term solution, as opposed to a golden Band-Aid, would link farm policy to
the fiscal and monetary environment in which American farmers
operate. The expansive decade of the 1970s is over and will not
return in the foreseeable future. There must be a restructuring
of family farmers' debts so that they can bring their agricultural
practices in harmony with the foreign and domestic economic realities of the 1980s.

A rational farm program would enable commercial family
farmers to produce for actual world need at prices that cover the
cost of production. Surperfarms should be moved to the back of
the line for government support programs. Congress must re-
write the tax code so that it rewards farmers for working the land,
not the tax system. We are heirs to a family farm system that is
the most productive, innovative and efficient in the world. We
owe it to future generations to preserve it.

HOW WE'RE GONNA KEEP 'EM OFF OF THE FARM[2]

Do we have a moral obligation to save the family farm? My father and uncle believed they were saving farmers when they
founded Sunray Fertilizer Company in the mid-1950s. Not only
were they first to bring anhydrous ammonia to Iowa, but they
were the first emissaries of what became the Green Revolution.
It took them years to bring farmers around. These farmers were
not agricultural-college graduates. They were not regular read-
ers of the farming journals—they had too little time for that. Nor
had they been loosened up and made receptive by county extension courses, which were taught by people who at the time either
worked with impoverished families or gave cooking classes. Neither had the local farmers any direct contact with the expanding
network of agricultural scientists. The Mueller brothers were
missionaries, in every sense of the word, to this dubious group,
who were suspicious of all things unnatural or scientific; and of

    [2]Reprint of an article by William Mueller. Reprinted by permission from *The American Scholar*, 56:57-67. Win-
ter '87. Copyright © 1987 by *The American Scholar*.

course liquid nitrogen, as anhydrous ammonia is called, is as unnatural as it is possible to get: pressurized, so cold it burns, able
to blind you in moments. Many farmers thought the Mueller
brothers were stark raving mad.

My father and uncle had a vision. Certainly they hoped to
earn some money from Sunray Fertilizer, but there was so much
more at stake here. Both brothers had been born in the back
room of a farmhouse. They lived with slime, mud, death, blood,
rust, decay, and manure. Always manure. Manure is what distin-
guished country boys at school. Manure is what city boys pointed
out about their country cousins: shit kickers. Blessed with intelli-
gence and drive, these brothers would look closely at a system
that claimed the life of their sister and gave their father nothing
back for his years of hard work except free and clear title to the
land; and it made the brothers dream of faraway businesses and
faraway careers.

While in the prosperous business of selling bottled gas in Ce-
dar Rapids, with a virtual monopoly in the town, my uncle
learned of this new stuff, this petroleum by-product the gas industry had concocted, called anhydrous ammonia. Without even
waiting for the scientific reports, which his agricultural mind well
understood already, he shared his dream with my father. The
brothers would seek out the epicenter of rich farmland—Hardin
County, Iowa—to begin the grand experiment. They saw it as de-
liverance from the mire, from the manure, from nature's
limitations. They would offer farmers the means to redefine agriculture.

Of course farmers came around to accepting liquid nitrogen.
In fact, when yields began shooting up, farmers reacted exactly
the way a drug addict would respond: they begged for more, far
more than the soil tests indicated. The revolution spread. Sons
were dispatched to agricultural colleges, data began streaming in,
and the vast petrochemical industry realized they finally had the
ultimate pigeon. Liquid nitrogen would spawn a constellation of
allied developments in farming whose cumulative effect was to
place farmers on an ever-narrowing path. Certainly if ever anyone was being saved, during this period it was the family farmer.
Because of liquid nitrogen a farmer could boost his yields by 100,
even 200 percent. Because of liquid nitrogen he could use those
profits to buy more land. Because of liquid nitrogen and the
chemicals that followed, he could farm far more than he ever had

before. And because of the chemically dependent farmstead, he could at last operate commercially on a large scale—not simply getting by, but earning good money and raising kids *and* accumulating assets for the future. No longer pulling a manure spreader, he embraced the latest technology.

Farmers scrambled to become big-time operators, and that scramble included what agricultural historians saw as the last shakeout of farming's obsolete. Between the 1950s and the 1960s, *seven million* part-time and tenant farmers would leave. Taking their farm families with them, these obsolete farmers moved to small rural towns or went a little farther, to urban centers. Most of them became the backbone of the blue-collar class in the Midwest. From their time on the farm they had learned values that served them well in other fields. Their lands were now farmed by a shrinking nucleus of serious commercial family farmers, around whom grew a matrix of services, agencies, industries, and research centers that eventually represented one-fourth of the entire work force in this country. As each support group made its presence known to the farming community, it maintained that its express reason for existence was to save the family farmer.

It is difficult to establish precisely the point at which all these efforts to save the family farm soured. Farmers were quick to rename themselves "managers" and to develop "sound management practices." The terms are important here. Farming has historically been not merely a trade but a way of life, one based on moral and ethical principles. The American farmer is simply not erudite in voicing the transcendent value of what he is doing; he tends to think in more mundane terms: history, tradition, natural necessity, pride, respect for the past. These were qualities that the Mueller brothers encountered in trying to peddle liquid nitrogen. They had to overcome a legacy based on the notion that you respected forces greater than yourself. But the term "manager" detached farmers from their commitment to the ethics behind land and livestock. To manage is to control. To manage is to be responsible. To manage is to follow rules that are in existence for a reason. You do not need to explain to the family or neighbors why it was necessary to destroy the 110-year-old barn—good farm management required it. You do not have to explain why you are moving to wider corn rows and buying a huge four-hundred-horsepower tractor and renting out an additional six hundred acres of land: it is simply good farm management. Nor are ethics involved in the confining of hundreds of hogs. You guessed it: that is good farm management.

What was going on was that farmers were trying to separate the way they farmed from the act of being a farmer. They presumed that, like factory workers or office employees, they could be innovative with their acreage while remaining family farmers at home. Which is to say, they could still have the values of family farming: believing in the work ethic, remaining stewards of the soil, appreciative of history and family, lovers of nature, and innocent. Honest. Neighborly. Solid. It was precisely to save these things and perpetuate them forever that farmers undertook the revolution of their profession, accepting the tools and methods handed to them by such services as those the Mueller brothers and others who followed them provided. With each choice, however, came a trade-off, a moral confrontation that may have been completely ignored at the time.

Today the remaining farmers realize that not only has the way farming gets done changed, but so has the institution of the family farmer. In freeing farmers from the powers of nature, those who would save the family farm have only insured that the farmer serves them. Each new effort to save the family farm really means a non-farm benefactor profits while farmers lose not only income, but their principles. Each step now takes farmers further away from their heritage, making them more like those they despise.

The question one needs to address is not so much whether we have a moral obligation to save family farms as units as whether we have an obligation to preserve the family farm way of life. As economic units, family farms can also include very small farmsteads, where one or both adults hold off-farm jobs. The economics of farming today encourages both of these possibilities for the farmer. What I am suggesting is that, with increasing regularity, it is difficult to act in ways that encourage the family farm environment. Both for small farms that have significant off-farm income and for very large farms that are diversified, there is tremendous advantage in exploiting the farm economically. The large operation can install single-purpose farm buildings, such as hog confinements, that are eligible for rapid depreciation allowances. The farmer raises hogs, in other words, not because the world needs pork or because he has a better way to raise pigs, but because he can use the tax credit against profits in another area.

The small farmers have not shown any profits since the 1970s, but their number continually grows. Why? Because the net losses sustained on the farm lower one's taxes on off-farm earnings. In calendar year 1982, farm profits were estimated at $7.7 billion, while losses for tax purposes were $19.0 billion; and off-farm income amounted to 105 percent for these same farmers. Similarly, federal subsidy programs lure farmers into planting the same overproduced cash crops year after year.

The temptations to "federal crop" in unethical ways are tremendous, particularly for the large and medium-sized farmer. Price-support systems have been exploited by unethical farmers who plant poorly germinating field corn (not expensive hybrid seed) and receive compensation on the amount their yield is below the county average. That scheme drives down the total county average and penalizes their honest neighbors for overproducing, in which case they lose guaranteed payment. Other large farms buy up neighboring wood lots that have been nurtured for decades, contract them out to loggers, reaping an investment credit, and then declare that the razed ground was intended for cash crops, but they will hold them out of production—for which the government pays them. That's blackmail. The latest scheme began when the 1985 Farm Bill introduced the whole-herd dairy buy-out. By a stroke of luck, the program takes eighteen months to complete—just enough time for unscrupulous dairymen to bring to maturity thousands of heifers they will claim were going to be their dairy stock, which everyone knows would have been culled from the herd otherwise. What would have been veal or hamburger then earns that farmer an annual income for five years, as he is paid *not* to milk a cow he never planned to milk.

Of course not every farmer wants to exploit the system. Yet today the majority of family farmers struggle to stay free from compromise. It is becoming increasingly difficult to farm honestly and make a living at it. Those family farmers who follow their ethical principles are the ones now being forced off their farms. Because they believe in the work ethic, these farmers try to avoid becoming welfare cases. They will work mightily to produce corn that costs them over three dollars a bushel to grow, but that sells for a dollar less on the open market. In the process they become the kind of farmers they have detested all their lives. Whereas years ago they would have rested their land in pasture, they now continuously plant corn. They will put off tiling wet spots; they

sts of agribusiness or super-farm owners and often h₂
demise of family farmers. USDA has opposed alternati
ltural research. USDA has done little to help farmers de
kets. USDA has always had a cumbersome and self-se
m for distributing to farmers its research findings. Bu
cult to conceive of anything generated within the g₀
t more harmful than the 1985 Farm Bill that will be enf
period of five years. Critics of the bill, such as Senator
kin of Iowa, estimate that the provisions in it will force
ercent of all family farmers out of business before it ex
ndependent study conducted by the Office of Techn
ssment found that this bill, in conjunction with other f
encing farming, will, by the year 2000, eliminate a n
e 2.2 million farms we now have. What will be left is
00 large farms producing 75 percent of all food, and th
be small farms used for residences, alternative pro
farms, and of course as tax shelters. As is now the case
dies will be largely given to the largest farm units.

he current legislation has three areas that are partic
ful to family farmers. The crop-subsidy provisions
low compensation to farmers in comparison to market
eir grain. By signing up to limit their production, the
ling that market values for grain will stay depressed an
will get just enough from a subsidy check to make ends
ay off interest on their loans. But, for large farmers, t
ions on planting are lifted when they exceed the 90(
and they can both receive payment and hedge with
planting.

shed by environmentalist groups, the 1985 Farm B
d the Conservation Reserve Program (CRP), which is
to turn seventy-five million acres of erodible farmlan
e and timberland. But response to the program by fa
en very poor. They were obliged to submit bids to th
nt on what it would cost them to take their acres out o
n and seed the ground with cover from USDA's app
nds were rationed on a county level, and farmers in es
gainst one another, with low bids receiving the av
A regularly pits farmers against one another in this
ne-fifth of the eligible acres were represented in the
sponse, with bid levels unacceptable to USDA.

will no longer build terraces; and they cannot afford the luxury of seeding down a winter cover to protect against wind erosion. End rows and the margins of creeks and other wild habitats will be plowed up for those extra bushels they can produce. Some desperate farmers will take one-time gambles on high yields and use even more chemicals, which further damage the soil and contribute to an already chronic pollution problem. Others who cannot afford chemicals will farm by neglect, accelerating erosion and inviting plagues of pests and weeds. These stewards of the soil look over their handiwork with shame and anger because of their lack of choices. This is not the legacy they had envisioned for their children.

It is difficult to say which case is more tragic: the family farmer who recognizes the corruptions of the system and learns how to exploit food and land to his advantage; or the farmer who persists in being the kind of farmer he admires, who is systematically ground to dust. Many of the latter will never understand why they failed. They equate twenty-hour days with a man's worth. They look at their value within the society and believe that, if there is a fair God somewhere, then they ought to be paid. Their ethics are such that even though they readily see their value in the system, they are loath to accept charity. Again and again they plea just for a fair market price. They lament how hard it is to earn a living in this system.

Thus to the end they can be easily exploited by those who claim to save the family farm, but who instead only serve their own interests. Out of their sense of responsibility, these ethical family farmers have again and again been misled. They purchased land because bankers told them it was wise to leverage themselves into a higher debt structure. They bought new equipment because agricultural experts told them that to buy this year was the only shelter against next year's inflation and that expansion was the way of the future. They believed in those things. They applied their share of what is an annual ten-billion-dollar farm chemical bill, putting the liquid nitrogen on their fields, and tried to sort through the cacophony of dissenting voices that steered them to and fro.

Adding to the confusion has been the fact that the intent of those who serve agriculture has nothing to do with the malignancy of the outcome they achieve. Like the Mueller brothers, virtually all agricultural scientists labor for five, ten, or twenty years on projects to save the family farmer. I recently spoke to one of the soil scientists who as a young man got in on the early anhydrous ammonia research. At that time the excitement within his group ran high. Now, like many of the eight thousand other scientists within USDA, he is greatly disillusioned and troubled by what their work engendered. Theirs is good science gone bad; honorable men who overlooked the use of their work for wrongful purposes. Today, across the country, a group of scientists is trying to reverse some of this by developing alternative agricultural techniques. But the whole process of agricultural science is ideally structured to be exploited by service industries. It plods forward slowly, demanding infinite retesting and analysis. Meanwhile some of its findings are snatched up by industry to be rushed into the field, while others, which favor farmers over processors and agri-industries, will grow only in out-of-the-way agricultural stations and be reported in obscure official publications.

The release of agricultural advances saves the family farmer in theory, but it destroys thousands of farms in reality. The most recent example of this involves the introduction on the market of genetically engineered bacteria that stimulate a bovine growth hormone, resulting in dramatic increases in milk production. This bacteria will increase production from 10 to 40 percent for the cattle subjected to it. This comes at precisely the same time that the government is prepared to spend $1.8 billion to buy out dairy herds. The combined effect of these separate events will be to convince small family farmers to get out of the dairy business while huge corporate dairy farms thrive—precisely the opposite effect that scientists envisioned when they began work on this bacteria years ago. Good science, bad timing.

Entwined with the well-intentioned, if toxic, efforts to save the family farm are some insidious strategies to bleed them until they perish. One needs to begin with the four vast grain cartels that manipulate prices in so many ways that farmers are knocked completely out of the supply-and-demand formula. Consider 1983 when the government's Payment In Kind (PIK) program idled nearly half of all production acres. That same year the Midwest was hit with its worst drought in a decade. Yet at year's end, prices were stable for corn and beans, and the USDA reported there was *still* a surplus on hand. How could that be? The National Farmers Organization discovered that millions of metric tons of grain were imported by the grain cartels to create an artificial sur-

plus. That year marked the end for tens of thou while the non-farming public fumed over "welf: same predatory mentality has existed with farr chemicals as well as with the financial services public sector.

What disturbs farmers most is the growir predatory agricultural services have been aid long-trusted farm institutions. For decades, the worked with individual farmers to educate th bring to smart farmers methods that would farmers, and to help raise the quality of life for the Extension Service is computer-operated, l ing seminars and group meetings where th measured by head count. Each agent has to his or her time was spent; and the software fc as the data that the agents can deliver to the controlled by federal bureaucrats. An agent recognized for his effectiveness recently quit find nothing within the Extension literature t who wanted to use low-chemical, organic far the time he spent with these organic farmer his superiors to be wasted time. Similarly, far children off to agricultural colleges only to di ern methods destroy three generations of ca tragic of all is the realization that thousan have made agonizing decisions to bend to th to grow larger, to cultivate intensively, to "corruption"—and they are still destroyed year, even the "luxury" to accept corruptic farmer) has been removed for many family the farmer's character to continue working ment has been sold and the sheriff stands wi he is finally free of our efforts to save him

The identity most people assign to the "Do we have a moral obligation to save fami eral government. It is clear that the permai ed to serve farmers are not working. Repea in Congress have dragged bureaucrats c hearings and asked, "Whose interests does criminal fashion these public servants hav even in the face of staggering evidence th;

ter
the
ric
ma
sys
dif
me
for
Ha
40
An
Ass
infl
of t
50,
will
truc
sub

har
ve
for
gam
they
and
stric
leve
tion;

clud
tuall
past
has b
ern
duct
list. F
bid a
(USL
ion.)
ers' r

What is disturbing here is not simply that the government has once again miscalculated America's farmers. Within the conservation provisions there is also the stipulation that farmers reduce their soil erosion and nonpoint pollution of the environment. The Conservation Reserve Program in effect says to farmers: we are offering you what we think is a solution to soil erosion. Now that farmers have rejected this, the long-ripening adversarial conflict between the farming community and environmentalists will begin to erupt. Farmers who of necessity must farm their land in ways that cause erosion and pollution will now be environmental outlaws. The evidence against them will be clear, and EPA will move in to force compliance. Should this become a regulatory issue, with fines and sanctions attached, I have no doubt the family farmer will once again suffer.

Most perverse in the 1985 Farm Bill is the Dairy Reduction Program alluded to earlier. Here, counties are allotted a lump sum, based on their production of milk, and dairymen again bid against one another to capture some of these funds. The government is hoping to rid us of more than a million cows by the end of an eighteen-month period, which will allow the government to ease out of the milk price-support business. So far, the predictable has occurred. There is very little sign-up among the larger dairy producers and considerable sign-up with those small, family farm operations. In other words, family farmers are sending their cows to slaughter, while the serious producers who already overproduce milk are waiting to cash in on deregulation. So much for saving family farms.

Remember, too, that dairymen who agree to get out of the business for the five years stipulated do not have a wide range of alternatives. The relation of land size to income in dairy farms is unique. These farms exist best where other kinds of farms do not, usually in more rocky soil. Neither are dairy sheds very useful for the way beef or hogs are raised today. And of course dairy machinery is of no use without a cow attached to it. These small farms will have a very hard time indeed converting to grain or other livestock operations—without the great obstacle of taking on additional debts. Many of them are now signing up for the program because it offers quick revenues that come at a time when they have no credit or face additional investment costs to stay in the dairy business.

I think this buy-out of dairy cattle is a perfect metaphor for the full range of governmental programs offered to the farmer. Invariably when the government offers some assistance, it does so with provisos, with corrosive repercussions, and so positions the assisted farmer that he immediately becomes an adversary to other farmers. In this case, the appearance of more than a million cows on the market drives down the price for beef cows and affects hog prices as well. It also attacks the fundamentals of farming. Here are dairymen, who may be third or even fourth generation in the business, who deal with their cows from ten to fifteen years; their artistry is in understanding their animals more intimately than their competition does—a challenge they heartily embrace. They have culled from the line the lesser cows and kept the superior ones. They have watched their cows and know the moods of each cow in her seasons. They have sat up all night with a cow to turn a calf inside, and they have applied healing salves to her torn udder. And, should anyone suggest that the cows do not understand their place in the scheme of life, I would have them sit with me in my office each afternoon as the cattle, who are twenty yards away at the fence and listening to my radio with me, turn toward home. They do not need the beginning of "All Things Considered" to tell them the time. The same cow always leads and the rest follow, across the creek and up the hill and even into the stanchions—the same ones each morning and each night.

Consider, too, how this is all being handled. After making the choice to abandon your way of life, you are obligated by the government to *brand on the face* these lifelong friends. Then you take them down to the market where the buyers, mindful of your contractual agreement, have been offering as little as one-fifth the value of beef cattle, or a dime a pound. If this were not bitter irony enough, the government masterfully unveils its plan to support and subsidize an Irish investment group that is setting up a twenty-thousand-cow dairy operation in Georgia. Every drop of milk will be bought by the government. It does not save family farms to toss them lifelines to which are attached non-negotiable contracts requiring them to take the next step toward quitting farming altogether.

It is often suggested that the loss of family farmers witnessed in the past several years, which will culminate in a system devoid of them sometime around the year 2000, is a natural evolution.

What distinguishes the current exodus from those of earlier periods, such as those of the Southern sharecropper, the Appalachian tobacco hand, or even the Midwestern tenant farmer, is the context. Sharecroppers were not more efficient than the methods that replaced them. But family farmers are the most efficient farmers in the world. Tobacco hands were not as innovative, flexible, or cheap as the machines that took their place; but family farmers have the lowest operational costs of any size farming unit; and the typical family farmer has the skills of a dozen trades, crafts, and professions. Finally, those earlier displacements resulted in continued cheap goods for the consumer.

Evidence suggests that if control of food is concentrated into fifty thousand units around the country, food prices will soar. At this time American consumers pay 12 percent of their disposable income for food. Were it not for family farmers, who shun billions of dollars in set-aside grants each year because, as one farmer told me, "Getting paid to not farm is not what I am about," control of produce would drive prices much higher. Were it not for family farmers, erosion and nonpoint pollution would reach the critical state. Because of family farmers there are hundreds of commercial banks still in existence, which could just as easily have been closed down if more farmers had filed bankruptcy or withheld repayments. The family farm has saved us, not the other way around. They exist despite our efforts to "save" them; but each new effort, like the 1985 Farm Bill, must sound to them as Santa Anna's trumpets sounded to the fading defenders of the Alamo.

Americans have distanced themselves from the ethics and morals of food production, save where it serves them to think nostalgically about family farms as the source of our better values. Little wonder that the *New York Times* poll finds a majority of Americans seeing farm life as superior to any other kind of life in this country. As consumers, Americans have enjoyed relatively inexpensive food. What will we do without the family farmer to watch over the system for us, to be our dupes and to create that pleasant situation through their own great discomfort? The government, in its Farm Bill and USDA leadership, is indicating that it will deregulate farming after it has finished destroying it. Consumers will be left with farms that are owned by absentee investment consortiums, insurance companies, or groups of professionals. Farming does not need ethics to continue. But farmers have always chosen this hard life precisely because it offered them the combination of making a living and living ethically. Until the Green Revolution, in fact, they had little choice but to be ethical. Now the ethical component is in danger of being lost, even while family farms are presumed to be saved.

A BUMPER CROP: AMERICAN FARM SUBSIDIES[3]

Those who till the soil are the chosen people of God.
                                                    —Thomas Jefferson

During the past two hundred years, Jefferson's maxim has become an integral part of American folklore and political rhetoric. Today, movies such as *Country* portray financially strapped farmers as victims of government policies—despite the fact that federal farm programs transferred an average of $12,000 to each farmer in 1983.

Obviously, the emotional support of the American public and the generosity of the federal government have not kept U.S. farmers from experiencing economic diffi lties. Farm incomes and land prices are down sharply, and there are few prospects of enough increased domestic food and fiber consumption, or of a surge in exports, to raise them. In 1985, when Congress returned to its quadrennial debate over farm programs, it received contradictory recommendations even from farm organizations: some urged the government to intervene more in agriculture, while others asked the government to phase out commodity programs.

Agriculture is often considered the crown jewel of the U.S. economy, the economic sector whose efficiency is heralded around the world. The record is indeed impressive: On a stable land base, American farm production has tripled since 1910 while employment in agriculture has fallen 80 percent. During the 1930s, average farm family incomes were less than half of average nonfarm incomes; today, many farm families earn as much as or more than nonfarm families, and most have much more wealth. But in the course of becoming so productive, the agriculture sector has been radically transformed.

[3]Reprint of an article by Elmer W. Learn, Philip L. Martin, and Alex F. McCalla, professors of agricultural economics at the University of California, Davis. Reprinted with permission of the authors from: THE PUBLIC INTEREST, No. 84 (Summer, 1986), pp. 66–78. © 1986 by National Affairs, Inc.

This article explains how American agriculture has evolved into a tripartite system of large farms, mid-sized and small "family" farms, and still smaller "rural residences." This changed structure means that federal farm programs, developed in the 1930s to assist family farms, today bestow most of their benefits on large farms. The article also explores a possible policy alternative which could redirect those benefits to the farms they were meant to help and fulfill the farm programs' intended goals.

Big Farms, Small Farms

A "farm" is officially defined as a place that sells at least $1,000 worth of farm products annually. In 1982 there were 2.4 million such farms, and the average farm family netted, according to *Agricultural Statistics,* $9,300 from farming. If farm families had only worked the farm, then, they would have had incomes lower than the poverty level. However, farm families averaged $16,400 each from nonfarm wages and salaries, dividends, and pensions, for a total annual income of $25,700. (In that same year the average U.S. family income was $24,200.)

But farm averages mask a considerable variation of economic welfare among farms, and it is more revealing to examine income and wealth when farms are divided into three groups: "rural residences"; "family farms," which can be divided into small and mid-sized; and large farms.

Half the number of all U.S. farms—1.2 million—sell less than $10,000 worth of farm products annually, and are considered "rural residences." In 1982 these rural residences together produced only 3 percent of all farm products. Rural residence families lose money farming, but their substantial nonfarm incomes and low living costs make them as well off as the average American family. Rural residence farmers average farm assets over $134,000. A few of these farms have struggling full-time farmers, but most are part-time diversions for retirees or persons employed full-time in other jobs. This group of farms receives 7 percent of federal cash payments to farmers.

About 112,000 large farms—equivalent to the number of farms in Minnesota alone—produce half the nation's food and fiber. These large farms, which sell more than $200,000 worth of farm products annually, average net farm incomes of almost $170,000 each. In 1982 the average large farm had assets worth over $2.3 million and an equity of $1.6 million. This group of farms receives 22 percent of the federal cash payments to farmers.

The remaining 1.1 million farms, each selling farm products worth $10,000–$200,000 annually, often fit the stereotype of the troubled "family farm." Half of these—one quarter of all farms—average sales from $10,000–$39,999; these small family farms on average lose $121 a year each, while together producing 9 percent of the nation's food. Small family farms have the lowest total family incomes, often because they are too big to allow the farmer to hold a full-time nonfarm job but not big enough to generate an adequate net farm income. Small farms average assets of $313,000 each, and together received 15 percent of all federal cash payments to farmers.

The other half of family farms sell farm products worth $40,000–$200,000 annually. These mid-sized farms include the 160–640 acre corn-soybean farms of the midwest, and usually require the part-time efforts of a spouse or children in addition to the full-time work of the farmer. Such farms together produce 40 percent of all farm products, but generate on average only $10,000 of farm income each despite average farm assets of almost $800,000—a return of less than 2 percent. Mid-sized family farms often include at least one non-farm worker, so the $21,000 average total income of this sub-group is close to the U.S. average. Together, mid-sized farms received 56 percent of all federal cash payments to farmers.

In sum, today's agricultural sector consists of 100,000 large and generally profitable farms, 1.2 million money-losing rural residences, and 1.1 million struggling small and mid-sized family farms. All share the name "farm," yet they have very little in common. It is hard to conceive of a realistic farm policy which can ever make rural residences and small family farms profitable, which means that 71 percent of all farms can be expected to lose money year after year. Helping family farms is also difficult because subsidy programs originally enacted to preserve a way of life wind up either increasing farm prices or financing the buying of surplus commodities from large farms. This federal assistance dilemma has its roots in the nature of the farm programs developed fifty years ago.

Why Farm Programs?

Farming differs from other production processes because of its biological character and its dependence on a relatively fixed supply of land. Since farming is land-intensive, it is dispersed throughout the nation; since the land supply is fixed, farmers must bid against other users to expand. During the 1970s, high farm prices, low interest rates (during a period of high inflation), new technologies, and tax laws encouraged farmers and nonfarm investors to bid up land prices. Rising land prices increased the wealth of landowners, and explain why some farmers lament that they "live poor and die rich."

Farmers produce essential food and fiber in a biological production process fraught with uncertainties. Weather and other unpredictable factors cause the supply of farm products to fluctuate, but the demand for food in industrial societies remains stable—the average American eats about 1,400 pounds of food annually regardless of farm prices. Consumers do shift between more and less expensive commodities as prices and incomes change, but such changes have relatively small effects. For example, despite extensive recent discussion about the harmful effects of too much red meat, the average American ate seventy-eight pounds of beef annually in the 1960s and seventy-seven pounds in the early 1980s. Because of this stable demand and fluctuating supply, relatively small commodity shortfalls or surpluses translate into large changes in the prices farmers receive for their products. Consumers usually do not appreciate the magnitude of such fluctuations because only one-third of the average dollar consumers pay for food reflects the price of the products farmers sell.

Public policies and competition among farmers have increased the supply of farm products faster than the demand for them. New seed varieties, improved pest controls, and better management methods developed by land-grant universities have increased agricultural productivity; public investments in infrastructure such as irrigation and transportation have increased farm output; and rising labor costs and the availability of nonfarm jobs have encouraged farmers to substitute machinery for labor. The result has been a chronic oversupply of farm products, which in turn has meant low farm prices and incomes.

The number of American farms peaked at 6.8 million in 1935, when one-quarter of the population lived on farms. Farmers had experienced low farm product prices and incomes since the 1920s, and books such as the *Grapes of Wrath* highlighted the misery of the farm sector which justified farm programs designed to increase and stabilize farm incomes.

Farm incomes can be supported directly or indirectly. Direct income support would entail having farmers produce and market their commodities and then report their incomes to the federal government. The government would then mail a check to the farmer for the difference between his actual income and a "fair" or "target" income. But farmers generally prefer "fair" prices to direct income support: direct subsidies are explicit, and nonfarmers might ask why farmers should have their incomes guaranteed by the government. So, federal farm programs sought to raise farm incomes indirectly by establishing minimum prices for basic farm commodities. In 1933, the federal government declared that wheat, corn, cotton, tobacco, rice, milk, and pork were basic commodities, and established programs that made the government the buyer of last resort for these commodities.

Fifty years later federal farm policies continue to establish minimum support prices for commodities such as wheat, corn, and rice. If farmers choose to participate in such programs, they pledge their harvested commodity to the Commodity Credit Corporation (CCC) in exchange for a year-long "nonrecourse loan" equal to the support price times the number of bushels. If wheat and corn prices rise, the farmer repays the loan and sells through private channels; if prices remain low, the farmer defaults and the CCC keeps the grain. Such minimum prices and loans are available for many other commodities, including cotton, rice, soybeans, wool, and honey.

In the case of milk, instead of loans, the federal government offers to buy unlimited amounts of milk products at announced prices, thus establishing a price floor for milk. In recent years, the federal government has been buying about 10 percent of U.S. milk products, storing them at an annual cost of over $2 billion, and disposing of some of the surplus through cheese giveaways.

Both loans and direct purchases make the federal government a last-resort buyer which acquires buffer stocks of basic commodities. If wholesale prices rise, these buffer stocks can be released to hold down consumer prices. If wholesale prices remain low, costs for buying and storing the surplus mount.

Money for Nothing, Wheat for Free

But a guaranteed above-market price encourages more production, so support prices have to be accompanied by acreage reduction programs. Thus, farmers who want CCC loans must also agree to "set aside" some portion of their acreage which normally would be planted with wheat or corn. Wheat and corn production, however, usually falls less than predicted because farmers idle their least-productive land and apply extra fertilizer to the planted acreage.

The federal government cannot easily buy and store perishable commodities such as fruits, vegetables, and milk, so it permits farmers to impose marketing restrictions on themselves. A tentative program ("marketing order") is formulated to regulate production standards, to raise funds for research and promotion, or to regulate the flow of the commodity to retail buyers. If a majority of the commodity producers approve, all producers must abide by the restrictions or face federal sanctions for violating them. Most of the forty-seven federal marketing orders limit themselves to promotion and the enforcement of quality standards, but a few, including the California-Arizona orange and lemon orders, restrict the flow of the commodity to U.S. consumers.

Most farm programs influence the supply of commodities, but the federal government also increases the demand for farm products by giving away or subsidizing food purchases through the Food Stamp and School Lunch programs in the United States and the Food for Peace program abroad. The Food Stamp program, which cost $11.2 billion in 1983, distributes to poor people coupons that can only be used to purchase food (although recipients do in fact trade them for other goods and services). The Food for Peace program donates surplus commodities to some countries and offers subsidized credit to others.

Support prices and acreage reductions are the basic features of farm commodity programs. By the 1960s, it was clear that the support price had become the floor price, benefitting farmers who chose not to participate and reduce their acreages. The Kennedy administration proposed a program that would have required all wheat growers to participate and reduce their production, but such mandatory supply controls were rejected by farmers.

Instead of imposing mandatory supply controls, Congress created a two-tiered price support system, providing commodity support prices lower than the previous ones (but still above the free market price) for all producers, and a new set of higher commodity "target prices" to those farmers who agreed to reduce their acreage. This system established incentives for farmers to join the program and curtail production, while retaining minimal price supports for those who did not. Several years after a few farmers received large cash payments—in 1967 five farmers each received over $1 million—limits were placed on payments to farms, and are now no more than $50,000 per commodity. This payment cap has kept most of the very large farms out of federal commodity programs.

Feast or Famine

The 1970s were the glory days of American agriculture. In the early years of the decade, a drought in the United States, energy price hikes and subsequent inflation, crop failures and policy changes in the Soviet Union, and devaluation of the dollar all prompted dramatic increases in exports, farm prices, and U.S. land values. Wheat and corn prices tripled between 1971 and 1974. Land prices rose 55 percent in the early 1970s and then doubled between 1975 and 1980. Farm exports jumped from $7 billion in 1970 to $41 billion in 1980, when the United States exported $24 billion more of farm products than it imported. Farmers and investors, convinced that the United States was the only country which could feed a hungry world, expected burgeoning exports to maintain high farm prices and land values.

The farm outlook dimmed in the 1980s, however, when Argentina, the European Economic Community, and other nations began producing and exporting more grains in response to higher prices. The strong dollar made American grains more expensive to developing nations mired in recession and debt. Farm prices fell as real interest rates reached historic highs, and the inflationary pressures that had propped up land prices and supported the mounting farm debt ebbed. The ambitious farmers who had expanded saw the value of their land shrinking, and they sought federal assistance.

Farm prices fell again in 1982, and still more farmers participated in government commodity programs. The direct costs of farm programs rose, and the government accumulated burdensome stocks of wheat and corn. When farmers pressed for relief, the Reagan administration responded in 1983 with the Payment-in-Kind (PIK) program, a massive acreage-reduction scheme. PIK transferred about $19 billion in cash payments and $9 billion worth of surplus crops to farmers who reduced their plantings. The PIK program was the most expensive farm program in U.S. history—in 1983, the average commercial farm received a transfer of almost $30,000 from the government. (Many commercial farms did not participate, so the average payment to participating farms was even larger.)

PIK was only a temporary respite for farmers. Farm prices sank further in 1984 and 1985, and interest burdens and declining land values pushed some troubled farmers toward bankruptcy. When Congress began a new debate over farm programs in 1985, it heard, as was mentioned earlier, contradictory recommendations. Almost all commentators agreed that current farm programs had become inappropriate for today's agriculture, but critics disagreed on whether more or less government intervention was required. However, one common thread running through the 1985 debate was the implications of the integration of American agriculture into the United States and world economies.

Growing Money

The price support and acreage-reduction mechanisms developed in the 1930s helped to transfer monies from the nonfarm to the farm sector and labor from farms to industry, back when farming was largely a domestic enterprise. Throughout the 1950s and 1960s, farm exports just exceeded imports—in 1969, the agricultural trade surplus was only $1.1 billion. In the early 1970s, exports surged, and the agricultural trade surplus rose to a peak of $26.6 billion in 1981. Today, the U.S. exports more than half of its wheat and cotton, almost half of its soybeans and rice, and one-third of its corn.

During the 1950s and 1960s, American agriculture was largely insulated from domestic and international economic policies. The domestic economy was relatively stable, and changes in the U.S. money supply had only minimal effects on the farm sector. Fiscal policies influenced the government's willingness to support farm prices and incomes, but the major impact of macroeconomic policies during these years was their effect on the unemployment rate: Farmers left agriculture when nonfarm jobs were plentiful.

Farming became increasingly integrated into the domestic economy through its reliance on machinery, chemicals, and other items, purchased from nonfarm suppliers. Historically, family farms had been independent enterprises that made many of the items needed to farm. This independence permitted farmers to "tighten their belts" when farm prices and incomes were low. But the share of farm supplies which were purchased began rising during the 1920s when tractors replaced mules, and jumped after World War II with further mechanization and the availability of new seeds and chemicals. Today, a farm operation is similar to a manufacturing enterprise: The farmer buys machines, seeds, and fertilizers, adds his labor and land, and sells the output.

U.S. agriculture was integrated into the international economy in the 1970s because of expanded exports and flexible exchange rates. The introduction of flexible exchange rates and the emergence of an international capital market meant that domestic policy decisions were quickly translated into changing interest rates and a new value of the dollar. For example, when the money supply was tightened in 1979, U.S. interest rates and the dollar rose, causing U.S. economic activity and exports to constrict in 1980–81. Indebted farmers were hurt in two ways—they had to shoulder higher interest burdens with commodities that were worth less.

During the 1970s, most American farmers got much richer because the value of farmland doubled from $500 billion to $1 trillion. The average commercial farmer enjoyed capital gains of $500,000, and many ambitious farmers borrowed money to buy more land. This borrow-and-buy strategy was rational and profitable during the late 1970s, when interest rates averaged 7 percent and land prices appreciated at an annual rate of over 25 percent. However, interest expenses rose with the mounting farm debt, so that those expenses exceeded income from farm assets by the early 1980s. With expenses greater than income, and few prospects of a surge in inflation or farm exports to push up land and farm prices, some farmers now face bankruptcy. This bankruptcy threat illustrates how today's farm problems influence the development of the detailed farm legislation that will prevail through 1989.

Economic Problems, Political Solutions

American farmers owe $210 billion: 35 percent of that amount is owed to the Farm Credit System, 25 percent to commercial banks, and the rest to insurance companies, other government agencies, and individuals. The Farm Credit System consists of twelve regional banks, each with a lending arm for land, short-term production loans, and farm cooperatives; observers predict that 15 percent of the system's $74 billion loans to farmers may be uncollectable. Predictions to record 1985 crops and continued low farm prices, farm debt problems, and the prospect of the 1986 elections soon turned congressional debate away from the Reagan administration's demand that the income transfers to farmers be reduced and towards congressional proposals for government bailouts of farm lenders. Despite a four-year farm bill enacted in 1981 that was predicted to cost the federal government $11 billion but actually cost $63 billion, the 1985 farm debate that began with intentions of reducing farm program costs soon turned into a discussion of whether $10 billion or $20 billion annually would be enough to save the family farm.

American farm programs that raise farm prices and idle acreage are counterproductive because other nations expand their farm production on the knowledge that U.S. farm programs establish price floors for wheat, corn, and other commodities that are traded. As Congress raises farm prices to help U.S. farmers and mandates acreage reductions to reduce farm program costs, Argentina and the EEC expand their production of wheat and feed grains. The United States is the largest exporter of such commodities, so congressionally established minimum farm prices become world prices, enabling foreign farmers to produce as much as they can under the U.S. price support umbrella.

The United States and Western Europe are net food exporters, while most of the developing nations of Asia, Africa, and South America are net food importers. The populations and eating habits of industrial nations are relatively stable, and farm productivity continues to increase, so the main hopes of U.S. and European farmers for higher prices are increased demand in the developing world or continued subsidies from the nonfarm sector.

Developing nations did dramatically increase their food imports in the 1970s, but their debt problems have forced them to reduce food imports in the 1980s. These nations are uncertain prospects for U.S. farmers because of limited foreign exchange, goals of food self-sufficiency, and irrational agricultural policies. For example, many African nations require farmers to produce and sell cotton or cocoa to a government agency which offers a below world market price. The government often uses this tax on farmers to import commodities which are distributed to urban consumers at subsidized prices. Such rural taxes and urban subsidies create incentives to migrate to the cities of the Third World, but the resulting congestion rarely accelerates economic growth.

United States farmers have an export market only if developing nations can export enough to earn the foreign exchange needed to buy U.S. commodities. If developing nations modify their farm policies, their own domestic production temporarily increases enough to reduce or eliminate the need for imported food. However, as incomes continue to rise, consumers switch from bread and rice to meat and other livestock products, so the industrializing nations such as Korea and Taiwan have emerged as major markets for U.S. soybeans and feed grains. Still, most developing nations have not adopted the agricultural policies necessary to increase food production or promote industrial sectors that can earn foreign exchange needed to import U.S. grains, so an expanded market for U.S. commodities in such countries frequently depends on food aid.

As long as export markets in developing nations remain uncertain, American and European farmers must look to taxpayers for subsidies or face a restructured agricultural sector. European farmers are guaranteed higher-than-world prices for commodities such as sugar, dairy products, and wheat, and the European Economic Community spends two-thirds of its budget to subsidize exports of the surplus. American farmers receive loans and cash payments in exchange for reduced production, and they have maintained substantial political clout despite their diminished numbers. This political power is reinforced by alliances with rural bankers, fertilizer producers and machinery companies, and food processors. As Congress began to debate the farm bill in 1985, stories of farm bankruptcies convinced 65 percent of the respondents in one poll to agree that it was a "bad idea" to reduce farm aid in order to cut the federal deficit. Some farm organizations continue to demand government-supported prices that are 100 percent of "parity"—meaning that a bushel of wheat should have the same purchasing power today that it had between 1910 and 1914. Even though farm subsidies transfer tax monies to a group with above average incomes, the ability of farmers to retain their subsidies cannot be underestimated.

What Are Our Real Goals?

The political process has continued price and income subsidies because farm policy has no clearly articulated goals. In earlier decades there was much discussion and debate over farm policy goals and alternative means of achieving them. However, during the 1985 debates, goals were rarely mentioned or debated. Clarifying three traditional goals—saving family farms, assuring an adequate supply of food, and preserving land and water for future generations—illustrates how farm policy might be reformed.

Although preservation of the "family farm" has been the favorite catch-phrase of politicians and farm policy spokesmen for more than half a century, present policies do not preserve family farms. Furthermore, the United States is not closer to a precise definition of what a family farm is than it was fifty years ago. Most definitions of family farming stress three features: a farmer owns or is buying the land being farmed; a family lives on and manages the farm; and the farm is operated with little or no hired labor.

During the 1930s and 1940s American agriculture was comprised largely of farms that satisfied one or all of these conditions. Today the picture has changed. Over half of the nation's cropland is farmed by someone other than the owner; almost half of all farmers report that they are primarily engaged in a nonfarm occupation; and hired workers do about 35 percent of the farm work. Price support programs do not forestall further movement away from the traditional family farm, and may actually hasten it.

Provision of adequate supplies of food and fiber at reasonable prices is another traditional goal of farm policy. But even the complete elimination of price support programs would not threaten achievement of this goal. Despite production restrictions, the United States produces enough for domestic needs and has a surplus of 30 to 40 percent to export. Most farmland will remain in production even if farm prices go down further. In spite of the financial problems that have plagued American agriculture during the past few years, there is no evidence that any significant amount of farm acreage has been idled, suggesting that adjustment to changed market conditions is reflected in reduced land prices rather than by leaving land idle.

Long-term preservation of land and water resources is a third goal that can be traced to Theodore Roosevelt's administration. Current commodity programs, however, work against this goal. By encouraging maximum yields per acre and by failing to discourage "sod-busters," commodity programs have encouraged the farming of highly erodible soils. Furthermore, these programs are at best indifferent to extensive use of irrigation and chemicals. Irrigation threatens the long-term stability of some aquifers, and chemicals threaten the quality of the water in rivers and reservoirs into which water from irrigated acres drains.

A farm policy which addresses these goals could include an income assurance program for family farmers, maintenance of the public research system, and elimination of acreage controls. Some family farms might be preserved by a policy that provides "income assurance" targeted specifically to family farms. Income assurance could mitigate the effects of low farm prices by bringing the incomes of eligible family farmers part of the way toward a target income. The program might, for example, operate only for mid-size farms, those with gross sales between $40,000 and $200,000. If properly designed, such a program need not preserve inefficient farms, because economies of size in agriculture are largely exhausted by farms that sell about $200,000 worth of products. However, the program would reduce for family farmers some of the financial risks associated with the inherent instability of agricultural product markets.

Long-term adequacy of food and fiber supplies is dependent more on public and private research than on commodity programs. Such research and related extension programs should continue, not only to assure domestic food supplies but also to maintain American agriculture as a world-class industry. The income assurance program could provide the means for farmers to innovate, and competition among family farmers and between family and larger farmers would create the incentive to apply new knowledge and techniques. If farm prices fall to market-determined levels, American consumers would continue to enjoy reasonable food costs. Furthermore, the price "umbrella" that U.S. policy has erected to shelter foreign competitors would be removed, improving trade prospects for American farm products.

Elimination of acreage controls would place less emphasis on land as the constraining resource in production, leading to more extensive use of land on all classes of farms. Provisions requiring appropriate soil and water use practices as a condition for participation in the income assurance program should be an integral part of a revised farm policy. Local and regional land- and water-use regulations should be strengthened to prevent nonconserving practices by other farm operators.

A transition to the free market which is cushioned by an income assurance program for family farmers is not a complete farm policy. But it does suggest a route by which we might move away from the commodity-based programs to a new set of policies more consistent with perceived goals and with the economic realities of a modern, international American agriculture.

U.S. FARM DILEMMA:
THE GLOBAL BAD NEWS IS WRONG[4]

America's farmers entered the 1980s feeling more prosperous and secure than at any time in modern history. They had just survived a furious onslaught of new farm technology, which helped to cut the proportion of farmers in the U.S. population to less than 4 percent. Overseas demand for food was being stimulated by economic growth. World trade in agricultural commodities had increased by some 10 million metric tons per year through the 1970s, and the United States had received most of the new business. Land values rose 50 percent in real terms during the decade.

If any farmers still had doubts about their future, the *Global 2000 Report*, which was presented to President Carter in 1980 and which was based on the best projections of the U.S. government,

[4]Reprint of an article by Dennis Avery, senior agricultural analyst, U.S. Department of State. Reprinted by permission from *Science*, 230:408–12. O. 25, '85. Copyright © 1985 by *AAAS*.

predicted that world demand for food would increase vastly in the next 20 years, that real food prices would double, and that developed countries would have to supply most of the increase. Conservationists immediately expressed concern about the tremendous pressure this food demand would put on the world's cropland. Some even suggested that resulting deforestation and erosion might alter world climate. Improved farm technology looked like a slender hope; yield increases were tapering off and higher oil prices threatened to expose our dependence on petrochemical-based fertilizers and pesticides.

Today, just 5 years later, the world of the American farmer lies in disarray, with mounting surpluses, heavy farm debt, and massive farm subsidy costs. Demand for U.S. farm products is weak, land values are down, and farm policy seems to be at a dead end.

Yet the long-term need for food is as critical as ever. The population continues to increase. Erosion and deforestation are still being reported. The worst famine in Africa's history has caused thousands of deaths and has malnourished millions.

The Bad News Is Wrong

The bad news for the American farmer is that the global bad news is wrong. The world is not on the brink of famine or ecological disaster brought on by desperate food needs. According to the Food and Agricultural Organization, world agricultural output rose 25 percent between 1972 and 1982 to reach an all-time high. Farm output in less-developed countries (LDC's) rose 33 percent. Compared to an increase of only 18 percent in developed countries (DC's), where markets were already saturated. Per capita food production rose 16 percent in South America and 10 percent in Asia. Equally important, the annual rate of growth in farm output in LDC's has been rising—from 2.7 percent in the early 1970's to 3.3 percent in 1977–1982. (The *Global 2000 Report* projected an overall farm productivity growth of 2.2 percent, with most of it in the developed countries.) The growth rate in the LDC's would have been even higher if the averages had not been skewed by some dismal farm policy failures in countries with good agricultural resources, especially in sub-Saharan Africa.

The improved performance by farmers in LDC's is basically due to improved technology and stronger incentives to use it.

The wheat and rice varieties of the Green Revolution are legend; genetics has gone on to produce the world's first hybrid wheat, cotton, rice, and rapeseed. Triticale, a hybrid of wheat and rye, outyields other cereals by 250 percent under certain unfavorable conditions. There are new sorghums for Africa that may have Green Revolution potential. Farmers in LDC's are also benefiting from better pest control technology, such as new low-volume pesticides and small electrostatic sprayers. Fertilizer use in LDC's has doubled and fertilizer production has tripled. LDC's tripled their real spending for farm research in the 1970's, and a global network of internationally funded farm research centers has been established with promising results.

Even Africa has the technology to double its crop yields and drought-proof its food supplies. The fact that this technology has not been more widely applied represents both a tragedy and an indictment of the farm and food policies followed by the African nations themselves.

The farm and food policies of the Third World are improving, however, prodded by population growth, and ironically, by the sharp declines in external financing for Third World governments. For the first time, the Third World is focusing on productivity rather than spending. The LDC's are also learning from the successful experiences of such nations as China and Malaysia. All of this is good news for the hungry of the world, but it will not ease the pressure on U.S. farmers.

Constraints Less Severe Than Expected

The constraints that were expected to limit food production during the 1980s and 1990s have been far less severe than almost anyone foresaw.

Cropland. One of the most obvious constraints is cropland. Most of the world's best and most accessible cropland is already in use. [Some nations, such as the Sudan, Zimbabwe, and Thailand, still have large areas of uncropped arable land, but much of it is far from consumer markets and lacks a transportation infrastructure.] Man still cannot create new land. However, many developments now under way have the same effect:

• New corn varieties are ready to double yields for small farmers in Central America and West Africa. New high-yielding varieties are raising the output of wheat, sorghum, cassava, peanuts, and most other crops.

• Irrigation has been expanding. Most of this is in the form of highly efficient, small-scale wells. Turkey, however, is building dams to irrigate 7 million hectares in the upper Euphrates Valley—an area equal to all the cropland in Nebraska.

• Wet areas are being drained. West Africa may become self-sufficient in rice production by shifting from upland to swamp rice production (this will require ditches, dikes, and disease control efforts).

• Brazil is opening up 50 million hectares of acid soils on the Cerrado plateau; lime and phosphate make the area productive and competitive.

• New ways are being found to farm the world's 300 million hectares of black, sticky vertisol soils, which occur principally in India, Australia, and the Sudan. Much of this land was not cropped at all in the past; some is now being triple-cropped.

• Australia has developed the "ley" system for farming its semiarid land. An annual legume crop is substituted for the normal fallow year, sharply increasing the forage supply and fixing enough nitrogen to raise cereal yields in the ensuing year 15 to 30 percent. Overall, the ley system increases the productivity of dry lands 30 to 40 percent. Spain, Portugal, and the North African countries are trying to adapt similar farming systems to their millions of semiarid hectares. The systems require sophisticated management but the long-term prospects are good.

• Argentina, which has huge tracts of prime land oriented to pasturing beef cattle, is gradually shifting to more intensive cropping of grains and oilseeds. The government last year abolished a 25 percent tax on nitrogen imports, and nitrogen use jumped 54 percent. Since 1980 the grain exports of Argentina have been increasing by about 1 million tons per year, and average yields of hybrid sunflower varieties have recently increased 25 percent.

• Peru has raised its rice production by 40 percent in each of the past 2 years with a new upland variety that tolerates the aluminum toxicity of the soils in the western Amazon Basin.

• Even the United States has been draining, terracing, and irrigating land and making other investments that add to our cropland base.

Erosion. Soil erosion has been both less severe and less detrimental to the world's crop yields than many expected. Conservation tillage and minimum tillage techniques have spread rapidly in many countries. Perhaps one-third of the Corn Belt is currently farmed with some form of conservation tillage, probably including most of the land at serious risk. The University of Minnesota Soil Science Department recently concluded that current rates of soil erosion, extended over the next 100 years, would cause irreplaceable losses in Corn Belt yields of less than 8 percent. Such losses would not be negligible, but seem certain to be dwarfed as we find even better conservation methods and improved production technologies over the next century.

Much of the world's cropland has a more serious erosion problem than the Corn Belt, of course. But raising the productivity of the best land relieves the pressure on fragile land. Steep and rocky land in New England and West Virginia has been relegated to pastures and forestry. Investments in drainage, land leveling, contour cultivation, and tree planting have made cropping safer on other land. The moldboard plow is disappearing from many farming regions.

In the developing world the productive potential of the best land has not been fully realized. Africa has the worst erosion problem in the world, yet plants a relatively small fraction of its arable land to crops in any given year. Traditional bush fallow periods range from 6 to 20 years. Population growth is now forcing shorter fallow periods, sharply increasing erosion rates. Most of Africa's food production takes place on millions of tiny subsistence farms with no fertilizer and seeds that are the horticultural equivalent of Indian corn. Overgrazing has been encouraged by communal land-holding and by traditions that give status to owners of larger herds of undernourished animals. A new sorghum hybrid has been developed in the Sudan that triples the yields of traditional varieties in much of East Africa and that is much more drought-resistant. A new sorghum for the drier conditions of the Sahel apparently can double cereal yields there. The International Potato Research Center has achieved test yields as high as 50 metric tons per hectare in Ethiopia—but few people in that poor country know what a potato is.

Oil prices. Oil prices are constraining agriculture much less severely than was expected as recently as 1981. Real oil prices have already dropped one-third from their peak and may well decline further. More efficient techniques are being developed for such energy needs as crop drying. Low-volume pesticides are effective in applications of less than 100 grams per hectare. The prices of petrochemical-based fertilizers never rose as much as oil prices because of relatively cheap natural gas produced in association with oil. Fertilizer is often the most attractive market outlet for such gas. Indonesia has increased its annual production of fertilizer from a few thousand tons to 1.2 million tons in the past decade, and is using most of it on its own crops. Such major oil producers as Iran and Nigeria are still flaring off large quantities of gas (although Nigeria is now building one medium-sized plant).

Running Out of Farm Science?

The pessimists assumed that the major discoveries which could sharply increase world agricultural output had already been made. Superficially, there was some justification for accepting this premise. Productivity gains in the United States and other developed countries had slowed in the late 1970s. However, progress in agricultural science has always been somewhat erratic. Over the longer term agricultural science has always moved forward in tandem with other areas of research.

Ongoing research throughout the world has produced a host of new developments that raise agricultural potential:

• The first genetically engineered vaccines. One prevents a major form of malaria, the other is the first fully safe weapon against foot-and-mouth disease. Both vaccines are made from the protein coatings of the disease organism, which triggers the immune reaction without risk of infection.

• The first viral insecticide, which attacks only the *Heliothis* genus of insects (corn earworm, tomato hornworm, tobacco budworm, soybean podworm). The spores of the virus remain in the field after the worms have been killed, and attack any succeeding generations.

• A weed, *Stylosanthes capitata*, turned into a high-yielding forage legume for the huge acid savannas of Latin America. The plant outyields the best previous forage crops in the region by 25 percent.

• Isoacids, a new class of feed additives for dairy cows. They increase bacterial action and protein synthesis in bovine stomachs, raising milk production or reducing feed requirements. The product is already being test-marketed.

• Embryo transplant operations to boost the genetic impact of top-quality dairy cows. The cows are given fertility drugs to induce multiple ovulation, and the fertilized eggs are then transplanted into the ovaries of average cows for gestation. The supercow can thus produce dozens of calves per year instead of just one. Thousands of such operations are now being performed each year.

• Short-season hybrids that have extended corn production 250 miles nearer to the earth's poles in the past decade. The grain is now being grown as far north as central Manitoba. East Germany has developed a corn hybrid and plans to shift its hog feed from imported shelled corn to a domestically produced mix of corn and cobs.

• The first practical hybrids for wheat, rice, and cotton. Hybrid alfalfa and rapeseed are at the field test stage. Triticale has recently outyielded the best wheats under difficult conditions, such as cool temperatures and acid soils.

• A system of agricultural research institutions for the Third World. The Consultative Group on International Agricultural Research (CGIAR) now has 14 research centers attacking farm production constraints. These centers produced the original dwarf wheat and rice varieties that launched the Green Revolution. The International Crops Research Institute for the Semi-Arid Tropics (ICRISAT), in Hyderabad, India, produced the potential breakthrough varieties of sorghum for Africa. The International Institute for Tropical Agriculture (IITA), at Ibadan, Nigeria, has produced a cassava that resists several endemic diseases, and thus outyields current varieties by three to five times. New peanut varieties from ICRISAT under test in India and Africa show yields several times greater than those of current varieties. The International Laboratory for Research on Animal Diseases (ILRAD), in Nairobi, Kenya, plans to launch a new vaccination program against Africa's tick-borne East Coast cattle fever within the next year. The International Center for Tropical Agriculture (CIAT), in Cali, Colombia, has produced varieties that double bean yields in Latin America. The International Maize and Wheat Center (CIMMYT), in Mexico City, has new white corn varieties that could nearly double yields in Central America and West Africa. The International Board for Plant Genetic Resources (IBPGR), in Rome, is preserving species. IITA is experimenting with alley cropping for African food production. The International Livestock Center for Africa (ILCA), in Ethiopia, is designing new farming systems that could sharply increase food production in Ethiopia's famine-wracked highlands. The latest miracle rice from the International Rice Research Institute (IRRI), in the Philippines, needs only two-thirds as much nitrogen and one-tenth as much pest protection as previous high-yielding varieties.

• Biotechnology, which may ultimately add more to farm productivity than any other development. Biotechnology has already produced the foot-and-mouth disease vaccine and high-fructose corn syrup. In the offing are such possibilities as ammonia-producing soil bacteria that farmers can plant to fertilize their crops, the first plant protein that is nutritionally complete for humans, crops with more built-in drought and pest resistance, and animals with better fat-to-lean ratios.

A Systems Break?

With productivity trends now so strongly positive, pessimistic arguments center on the possibility of "systems breaks"—sudden, sharp changes in external variables that affect agricultural success. In fact, however, high-technology farming has demonstrated tremendous capacity to adjust to sharp economic and environmental changes. It successfully overcame the oil crisis and its attendant escalation in fertilizer prices. It has surmounted the banning of the early persistent pesticides and their broad side-effects, such as the buildup of insect resistance.

Irrigation helps to drought-proof India and Bangladesh. Sudan's new sorghum seeds, in a year so dry that local varieties failed completely, yielded more than the local varieties do in a good year. Dams and drainage cut flood risks and convert swamps to cropland where necessary.

Technology can also broaden the range of production possibilities: Florida's most frost-prone citrus groves are going out of production; imports of frozen juice from Brazil now fill the gap when Florida's crop is hit, and the high prices that used to make the frost risk worthwhile no longer occur.

Neither drought in the Corn Belt nor massive crop failure in the Soviet Union nor the most severe drought in Africa's modern history have produced actual shortages of food in the world (although there have been regional shortages, complicated by transportation difficulties). Most significant, high-technology agriculture is producing more food per capita nearly everywhere in the world, despite the most rapid rates of growth in population and food demand in history.

High-technology agriculture could probably even take a significant degree of change in global climate in stride. Farmers already successfully cope with annual and seasonal weather variability that has far more impact on crop production than would even a major global cooling or warming trend. Any climatic change in the foreseeable future is likely to have only a moderate net effect on world cereal production, with some countries being helped and others hurt, but with the world retaining ample productive capability. Moreover, past changes in world climate have come over periods of centuries—ample time for breeding programs to adapt plants and animals to the new conditions. (There is no solid evidence that a global climatic change is taking place. Meteorologists say that, while overgrazing and deforestation play a part in the drought cycle of the Sahel, the broader African drought of 1983 and 1984 was too large to have been produced by human activities on the continent; rather, the drought was caused by a severe Southern Oscillation, a periodic global weather phenomenon that has often produced African droughts in the past.)

Famine in the Midst of Plenty

Africa's famine proves only that population growth has pushed traditional African agriculture to the limits of its productivity, even in good years. Any drought there now means hunger. The inevitable next drought will mean more deaths unless African agriculture can be modernized.

Fortunately for Africa, much of the technology for modernization is already available. New varieties of corn, sorghum, peanuts, and cassava are raising yield potentials from the Sahel to Zimbabwe. New farming systems promise help for Ethiopia and Nigeria. Improved pest control and new varieties are raising West African yields of cowpeas tenfold. A leguminous tree native to Central America (*Leucaena leucocephala*) is well adapted to many arid parts of Africa; it can be planted for timber and erosion control and is very effective in alley cropping, in which the roots of these trees planted in rows fix nitrogen for food crops planted between them.

Improved seeds are relatively cheap, and so are moderate levels of fertilization and pest protection for most farmers getting efficient off-farm support. Farmers increasingly use them because they cut per-unit production costs and raise the productivity of land and labor. Tree planting and improved crop rotations may cost nothing except some family labor. Desperately poor farmers become less desperately poor by using such improved methods.

The most serious constraints on African agriculture are those imposed by the national policies of African nations. Most of these nations achieved independence in the 1960s, when the popular development model argued that LDC's could skip agricultural development and move straight into modern industrialism. Even the countries that were able to export industrial products, however, were soon spending most of their new earnings to import food for growing urban populations. Ghana nearly destroyed one of the continent's most productive export agricultures with low prices and state-run farms. Tanzania forcibly gathered its small family farmers into collectivized villages, where their productivity sagged. Ethiopia's tiny agricultural research station 10 years ago produced improved varieties of wheat and sorghum; with a little fertilizer, they were capable of doubling yields on the small highland farms. The Mengistu government sent the seeds and fertilizer to its new state farms, where yields with the new inputs were lower than those at the peasant farms without them.

Only recently have African governments begun to recognize the need for agricultural research and farmer incentives. African agriculture is likely to make significant strides in the next decade, partly because Africans are learning from past mistakes and partly because they no longer have the financial backing to continue making them.

Declining Advantage of U.S. Cropland

American farmers have long believed that an important part of their competitive advantage lay in the nation's superior cropland and climate. Those factors now mean less because technology and investment are rapidly diminishing production constraints on other land in other countries.

Because of the advent of short-season corn, corn-growing potential can be expanded in Asia, Europe, and Latin America; even the Soviet Union is trying again to expand its corn production. The European Economic Community has greatly increased its output of rapeseed, sunflower seed, and field peas and other legume crops in order to displace soybean meal in its livestock feeds. Saudi Arabia produced 130,000 metric tons of wheat in 1975, and in 1985 is expected to produce 2.3 million metric tons. High wheat prices have turned the Saudi desert green. Palm oil production is rapidly expanding in the Pacific Rim to compete with soybean oil. Cassava from Asia competes with corn for the feed market. Sweden has a new seed treatment that makes wheat more winter-hardy, and already has its own grain surplus.

Agricultural output is becoming less a function of natural factors and more a function of the degree to which cost-effective technology is utilized. High land values today no longer mean farm prosperity; rather, like expensive machinery or chemicals, they just mean high production costs.

The real competitive advantages of U.S. farmers today lie in their high output per farmer and in the scientific and industrial infrastructure that supports them. The United States has the best-trained farm managers in the world—vitally important when a modern commercial farmer has to master a broad range of scientific, engineering, and business skills.

U.S. farmers also get exceptional support from off the farm. When export markets for feedstuffs expanded rapidly in the 1970s, the United States already had farm-to-market roads, railroads, farm equipment manufacturers, and food processors able to handle large volumes efficiently. The government had grain inspection and grading services with worldwide reputations. Agribusiness radically increased investment in unit trains, barges, and export elevators. (Canada and Argentina are still trying to get their export-handling capacity up to their farming potential—a decade after the opportunity appeared.) The United States also has outstanding research institutions, both government and private, to produce new technology.

These advantages will continue to be critically important, because world farm export markets will be fiercely competitive in the next decade. Production in LDC's is increasing rapidly because of technology, experience, and the need to feed populations and to service debts. This output is not only displacing imports but is producing some export competition as well. China, for example, is suddenly exporting cotton and corn.

Some middle-income countries, like Brazil and Argentina, are also under strong debt pressures to maximize their export potential. Others are doing it just to achieve economic growth for their swelling populations.

Finally, most of the DC's still maintain farm subsidy programs that stimulate additional farm output. The most significant of these is in the European Economic Community, which has increased the tax base for its farm subsidies by 40 percent in the last year and which will take Spain and Portugal into membership in 1986. Wheat yields in the community increased 23 percent in 1984, field pea harvests in France have jumped 50 percent in 2 years, and farm productivity in Spain could readily increase by one-third in the next few years.

Outlook for the U.S. Farmer

In the longer term, population increases and economic growth will increase the overall market for farm products. Protein foods will continue to increase their importance in international trade. New products will emerge—just as the soybean emerged to profitably occupy 50 million hectares of cropland. The agricultures that meet these emerging demands are headed for higher productivity, increasing affluence, and broader opportunity, but they are also headed for more competition.

The U.S. farmer is in an awkward position to compete for this long-term market growth. The strength of the dollar has raised U.S. farm price supports in recent years by perhaps 35 percent above the levels Congress thought it was establishing. This has provided a profit umbrella for competing farmers all over the world. (It may be technically impossible to effectively administer dollar-denominated price supports in today's world of volatile exchange rates.)

The U.S. share of world farm export markets has dropped significantly, in part because of our long-term policy of storing surpluses rather than selling them. In the past several years, the payment-in-kind (PIK) program cut U.S. production, further encouraging competitors. Grain can now be imported into the United States more cheaply than it can be bought here, while the annual cost of U.S. farm programs has soared from less than $1 billion to about $15 billion per year.

The current mechanisms of the General Agreement on Tariffs and Trade are weak and ill-suited to defending free trade for farmers. Renouncing farm exports, however, would mean renouncing export earnings—recently about 25 percent of U.S. farm income. This would cost hundreds of thousands of jobs on

U.S. farms and in farm-related industries, while worsening the U.S. balance of trade and weakening economic growth.

The U.S. farm policy of the future must be geared to competing for buyers who have more alternative sources of supply than ever—their own agricultures, competing agricultures all over the globe, and more synthetics and substitutes. This means that our policies must be designed to reduce costs per unit and to provide farmers with the latest technology. Strong efforts are also needed to lower trade barriers; this will not only be good for U.S. farmers but will help the world to benefit from fuller utilization of global comparative advantages. Researchers need to look at farmland not only in the traditional sense but also as a potential source of biomass and the various kinds of complex chemical feedstocks that could be produced from genetically engineered plant life.

One thing seems certain: the price supports, land diversion, and storage programs that have dominated U.S. farm policy for the past 50 years work against the U.S. farmer in a world of high technology and rising productivity.

IV. DEBATE OVER A NEW FARM POLICY

EDITOR'S INTRODUCTION

Debate over a new farm policy has intensified in the last few years following a series of initiatives by the Reagan administration. In 1983 the government instituted a $9.2 billion payment-in-kind program (PIK) to deal with farm surpluses. Under this arrangement, the government paid farmers with crops from federal storage in return for idling acreage. It was hoped that it would hold down cash payments while reducing stockpiles, yet outlays actually increased to $18.8 billion. By 1985 the administration drafted a much more radical proposal that would provide for a phaseout of farm subsidies over a five-year period. It was quickly opposed, however, by farm groups, who argued that the administration was "pulling the rug" out from under agriculture. Eventually, in December 1985, a Farm Bill was approved by Congress and signed into law by the President, but it was a considerably modified version of the legislation urged by the Reagan administration. Farm subsidies were reduced somewhat and some acreage was restricted from cultivation under a "sodbusting" provision, yet this bill, too, has had disappointing results. Rather than being reduced, financial assistance to farmers has risen dramatically. A new direction in farm policy is clearly needed, but economists and agricultural analysts are sharply divided over its nature.

Section IV addresses the issue of restructuring agricultural policy. It begins with Mark H. Crawford's article in *Business Week*, reporting on President Reagan's plan to bring American agriculture into line with "market economics." A second article, by Devorah Lanner in *The Nation*, deals with an alternative bill favored by farmers themselves. While providing for a gradual elimination of subsidies, it would keep production in line with demand through mandatory price controls, and it would aid smaller farmers in various ways, including a five-year moratorium on loan foreclosures by the Farmers Home Administration. The Farm Law of 1985, in its final form, included some features of this bill. An editorial from *Commonweal* calls attention to another legislative proposal, the Save the Family Farm Act, or Harkin-Gephardt bill, which is now before Congress. The bill would have the government give loan priorities to smaller farmers and limit price supports to those farmers with genuine needs. The final three selections are related and sequential sections in the booklet *The Farm Crisis*, produced and published by the Domestic Policy Association, a non-profit, non-partisan foundation. The first of these presents the case for a continuance of subsidies to farming, an industry that *is* special and needs protection. Taking a differing view, the next article presents the argument for redistributing government assistance, which has favored the superfarm, so that it provides aid to those most in need. A final article in this three-part series presents the case for the elimination of all price supports and conversion to a "market" economy.

PLAYING WITH FIRE:
REAGAN TAKES ON THE AMERICAN FARMER[1]

It could quickly become one of the touchiest political issues confronting Congress in 1985. Just as he did in his first term, President Reagan will start his second by calling for a dramatic change in U.S. farm policy. But this time Reagan is shifting course. Instead of advocating Band-Aid fixes like the payment-in-kind program, he will try to persuade the new Congress to slash subsidy programs that have bolstered farm income since the New Deal. The goal: to force farmers to make planting decisions on the basis of economic realities in the world marketplace rather than on artificially high support prices.

In the end, Congress is not likely to buy much of the Reagan plan, but two factors probably will impel it to move some distance in that direction: a widening consensus that current farm policies do not work and a growing realization that agricultural subsidies must be reined in to help cut the federal deficit.

Sparring. Despite multibillion-dollar subsidy programs, U.S. agriculture, which accounts for 22% of the nation's gross national

[1]Reprint of an article by Mark H. Crawford, *Business Week* staff writer. Reprinted from Ja. 14, '85 issue of *Business Week* by special permission, © 1985 by McGraw-Hill, Inc.

product, still has not rebounded from the recession. Chronic overproduction, falling crop prices, declining land values, heavy borrowing at high interest rates, the ravages of weather, and an erosion of exports caused by a relentlessly strong dollar—all still plague most of the farm belt.

Reagan, having won the overwhelming backing of farmers in his bid for reelection, is now risking their anger. Already lining up against the Administration plan are such powerful lobbies as the National Farmers Union, the American Agriculture Movement, and the National Milk Producers Federation.

In essence, the Administration wants to cut annual outlays for core farm support programs—projected at $14.4 billion in fiscal 1986—by as much as two-thirds. It would accomplish this primarily by drastically lowering the ceiling on price supports and reducing the amount of government credit available to farmers.

Sparring over the specifics is still going on between Agriculture Secretary John R. Block and David A. Stockman, head of the Office of Management & Budget, but both agree that current government subsidies have inflated U.S. farm prices and are making American commodities less competitive in world markets. Exports sop up about one third of U.S. farm production. But since 1980, they have dropped from 163.9 million metric tons to 143.6 million in 1984. While exports will grow slightly in 1985, lower world prices are expected to cut gross income 4%, to $36.5 billion.

For the U.S. to retain market share, farm price supports must be lowered, in Block's view. It is a painful process, and Block concedes it will mean larger farms and fewer farmers. But he has promised that he would not suddenly "pull the rug out from under farmers." He has proposed phasing down federal support programs over five years, keeping outlays at a high $13 billion annually in fiscal 1987 and 1988, then gradually reducing them to $5 billion to $6 billion by 1991.

'No-Program Program.' But Stockman's overriding budget agenda may force Block to go back on his word. Fearing Congress will intervene late to halt the cuts in price supports, Stockman wants to lock in related budget savings now by slashing maximum price support payments from $50,000 to $10,000 annually per farmer within two fiscal years. In total, Agriculture Dept. officials say, it appears Stockman wants to cut farm outlays to between $3 billion and $4 billion as early as 1988.

"What the Administration is talking about," complains Margie Williams, director of government affairs for the National Wheat Growers Assn., "is very close to a no-program program." In fact, Agriculture Dept. officials, wheat industry lobbyists, and congressional staffers contend that a $10,000 cap would leave vulnerable farmers at the mercy of the market and of Mother Nature. Wheat farmers, for example, currently get support payments of $1 per bushel, and given the average crop yield, they would reach that $10,000 limit by the time they harvested 375 acres of land, Williams notes. Typically, however, wheat growers farm at least 1,000 acres.

'Big Risk.' Equally discouraging to farmers is Stockman's proposal to cap crop loans at $200,000 per farm. No cap exists now. The loan program provides farmers with short-term financing based on a per-bushel loan rate set by Congress in 1981. Both the Block and Stockman plans call for cutting back this program so that farmers would receive perhaps only 75% of the average domestic crop price. Currently, Agriculture's loan rate covers 100% of variable costs, and farmers are allowed to forfeit their crop to the Commodity Credit Corp. in lieu of repaying the loan. "If the Stockman caps stick," says a Block aide, "Congress is not going to take the Administration's farm proposals seriously."

The Senate will make some effort to reduce both price guarantees and loan rates. But strong signals are coming from Senate Majority Leader Bob Dole (R-Kan.), Agriculture Committee Chairman Jesse A. Helms (R-N.C.), and Budget Committee Chairman Pete V. Domenici (R-N.M.) that a complete phaseout of price supports is unacceptable, no matter how it is packaged. With 22 GOP members up for reelection in 1986, the Senate leadership appears unwilling to risk a farm sector revolt.

While there is strong sentiment in the Senate for getting agriculture on a market-oriented track, making the shift in these hard times "is one hell of a big risk," says a Domenici aide. "We all think that lowering price supports and loan rates will have the effect of making farmers more competitive." But he worries that the Block and Stockman proposals might not lead to increased farm productivity or to expanded export volumes after all.

Dismal Record. The American Agriculture Movement and the National Farmers Union contend that the Administration's program has little chance for success as long as the dollar remains overvalued, Third World economies are weak, and high farm interest rates continue to erode farmers' cash flows. "The real problem," charges Robert A. Denman, a lobbyist for the National Farmers Union, "is the way Block has administered farm programs."

The Reagan Administration's record in managing farm production has indeed been dismal. In 1983 it instituted the $9.2 billion payment-in-kind program (PIK) in reaction to huge grain harvests. The idea was to pay farmers with crops from government storage in return for idling acreage. It was supposed to hold down government cash payments while reducing stockpiles. But government outlays soared to $18.8 billion anyway.

The Administration's new approach to farm policy also will draw opposition from bankers. In the last half of 1984, 37 agricultural banks failed because of economic woes in the farm belt. "We are in concert with the Administration's longer-term objective for assuring that our farmers can compete in export markets," says Weldon Barton, agricultural representative for the Independent Bankers Assn. But with more bank failures ahead, his organization will oppose any major reduction in farm programs.

Heavy Clout. For now, the Administration has the tentative backing of such formidable farm groups as the American Farm Bureau Federation, the National Corn Growers Assn., and the American Soybean Assn. But their support, based on Block's pledge of an orderly transition to a market-oriented agricultural policy and on an aggressive agricultural export program, may erode. "If they don't effect a transition, the shock may be too great even for some of the well-managed, healthier farmers," says Robert I. Nooter, the Farm Bureau's assistant director for national affairs.

Even so, Congress is under strong pressure from the budget deficit to make farm programs less expensive. Most likely, it will wind up rolling back farm loan rates somewhat and reducing price supports for dairy, grains, and other commodities. But whatever its final form, the Administration plan faces sturdy opposition on the Hill, where farmers still wield heavy clout.

A FARM BILL BY AND FOR FARMERS[2]

At last, there is a farm bill that promises to give new life to beleaguered family farmers, combat soil erosion—greater now than in the days of the Dust Bowl—and eliminate Federal subsidies. The Farm Policy Reform Act of 1985 is the product of a series of forums sponsored by Minnesota Agriculture Commissioner Jim Nichols and his Texas counterpart, Jim Hightower. Hightower calls it a farmer's bill written by farmers. As chair of the Democratic National Committee's Agriculture Council in 1983 and 1984, he brought farmers together to set their own policy rather than leave it to the Washington lobbyists, bureaucrats, academics, bankers and land speculators. In hundreds of meetings across rural America, they reached agreement on the broad principles of the bill. Nichols and Hightower then drew up a proposal that challenges longstanding tenets of farm policy.

Passage of the bill, which would set policy through 1989, could be crucial to the survival of America's most productive and most jeopardized farm sector: the middle-size, family-style operators, once considered economic models of agriculture. The farm recession, now in its fifth year, is deepening to a full-scale rural depression. About 263,000 farmers have gone out of business since 1981; on average, 1,600 go under every week. "We are literally in the eleventh hour," Hightower says. "It comes down to one key question: Are we going to have a system of hard-working, efficient, independent family farmers in this country, or are we going to turn control of our food supply over to a handful of conglomerates and superfarm combines?"

The bill has received support from a coalition of rural and urban Democrats. Introduced in May by Senator Tom Harkin and Representative Bill Alexander, Democratic deputy whip, it is emerging as the main alternative to the Administration's bill, which is all but moribund. Among the co-sponsors are Representative Lane Evans, who is taking the lead in the House Agriculture Committee, and Representative John Conyers Jr., who has pledged the support of all nineteen members of the Congressional Black Caucus.

[2]Reprint of an article by Devorah Lanner, a Washington correspondent for the Center for Investigative Reporting. Reprinted by permission from *The Nation*, 241:19–20. Jl. 6, '85. Copyright © 1985 by *The Nation*.

Of the plethora of farm bills circulating in Congress, this one goes furthest in restructuring the farm economy. Most other proposals, Republican and Democratic, are variations on a single theme: reduce farm prices to stimulate exports and retain subsidies (though at a reduced level) to placate entrenched interest groups. "So far, most of the farm proposals have been to lower prices so we can compete in the so-called free market," says Harkin. "There is no free market. We set the world price and it doesn't make a lick of sense for us to set prices so low we bankrupt our own farmers just so we can sell cheap grain to Russia."

President Reagan, who had enjoyed wide support among farmers, alienated many of them this spring, when he vetoed emergency farm credit legislation. When 2,000 farmers came to Washington to protest, they found that the Department of Agriculture had locked its doors to them. As a result, the initiative has passed to the Democrats.

The central element of the bill is a program that would keep production in line with demand, bringing to an end policies begun under Earl Butz, who, as Secretary of Agriculture from 1971-1976, encouraged farmers to overproduce for a speculative market. Farmers would vote in a nationwide referendum to limit the production of nine major commodities. If a majority approved, all farmers would be required to withdraw at least 15 percent of their land from tillage and practice strict soil conservation on the idled acreage. The bill's sponsors say that removing land from production would attack the present glut; then if the program is allowed to run its course, the price floor for farm products would gradually rise until they reach 90 percent of parity levels by 1999. In 1986 alone, farmers could see their income increase by anywhere from $10 billion to $21 billion.

But will farmers vote for mandatory production controls? "Farmers see that they have no choice if they are going to make it. They will vote for controls if put before them," says Minnesota farmer Don Grover, who has taken out advertisements praising the bill in his local newspaper. Surveys of farmers conducted in the past year reveal strong support for controls in return for higher prices.

In addition to raising market prices by curbing production, the reform bill offers other programs that would benefit family farmers. Its major provisions would:

- Eliminate Federal farm subsidies, thus slashing the deficit by as much as $20 billion. Subsidies tend to benefit large operators disproportionately, mainly bypassing the family farmer.
- Place up to 30 million acres of farmland most susceptible to erosion in a reserve. The land would be used for growing hay, or as pasture, forest or wildlife preserve.
- Set stiff penalties for "sodbusting," plowing up easily erodible or untilled land. The new farm policy would do much to eliminate the incentive to squeeze production from marginal soil, a practice many farmers engage in to meet rising costs.
- Require large operators (those with a gross annual income of more than $200,000) to let a greater share of cropland lie fallow in times of surplus than smaller holders do. This stipulation would maintain the family farmers' share of the market.
- Establish a five-year moratorium on loan foreclosures by the Farmers Home Administration.

The program would not only benefit family farmers; it would help revive small towns and agriculture-dependent industries—companies that make farm machinery, for example—which have been hit hardest by the farm emergency. John Conyers, who represents Detroit, says, "This bill will generate at least $30 billion per year in new economic activity and maybe twice that. That means increased demand for all types of products. I'm convinced that any real recovery has to start on the farm."

Although in the law's first year higher farm prices would cause a jump of about 4 percent in the nation's food bill, that represents less than 1 percent of total consumer spending. Increasing the price of wheat from $3.33 per bushel to $4.95 per bushel would cause a 2.6 cent increase in a loaf of bread, but it would turn things around for the wheat farmer and his suppliers. The bill allocates approximately $1 billion to Federal nutrition programs, protecting Americans who are most vulnerable to a rise in food prices.

As for farm exports, the volume in sales lost through lower production would be made up in higher prices per bushel. Because other exporting nations peg their prices to ours, they would probably increase their prices also. Higher farm prices for all would help large debtor nations like Argentina and Brazil fulfill their international obligations.

The reform bill may also turn out to be a powerful organizing tool. It is picking up support wherever news of it travels. In the past several months, the Minnesota Department of Agriculture has reported brisk sales of slide shows explaining the program. Dixon Terry, an Iowa dairy farmer and a member of the Iowa Farm Unity Coalition, is helping organize local townships and communities throughout his state. "I'm surprised about how receptive farmers are to mandatory controls," he says. "This bill is such a distinct departure from the past. It shows that there are real solutions within reach; it creates a vision of prosperity."

Among the bill's proponents are dissident members of the American Farm Bureau Federation, which supports the Administration's "free market" approach; conservative commodity groups like the Nebraska Wheat Growers Association and the Texas Corn Growers Association; a number of United Automobile Workers locals; conservationists, rural businessmen and small-town bankers; grass-roots farm organizations; and countless farmers whose primary allegiance is to the survival of their farms.

The Farm Policy Reform Act cannot by itself solve the farm crisis. The current tax code, which encourages overproduction and concentrated land ownership, is beyond its reach. Also, the bill's moratorium on foreclosures does not apply to the quasi governmental Farm Credit System, which carries 37 percent of the nation's $212 billion farm debt [see Jim Schwab, "The Shaky Farm Credit System," *The Nation*, May 11]. But the bill would give farmers a far greater return on what they produce, while ending subsidies. Higher crop prices would begin to reverse the decline in land values and recover the 77 percent of net farm income that has been lost over the past four years.

This could be the year in which Congress decides whether the family farm will live or die.

WHICH FUTURE FOR FARMING?[3]

"We regret to inform you that a review of your Farmers Home Administration loan account indicates the need to take ad-

[3]Reprint of an editorial article, *Commonweal*. Reprinted by permission from *Commonweal*, 113:547-8. O. 24, '86. Copyright © 1986 by Commonweal Foundation.

verse action." To the more than 65,000 U.S. farmers who, this year, face debt restructuring or foreclosure, this letter from the government's lending agency of last resort says it all. Their land, livelihood, and way of life are in jeopardy. Yet the economic collapse comes as no surprise. Agriculture, America's largest industry, is in serious condition. How serious is suggested not only by the recent record number of farm foreclosures since the Great Depression, but by the figures last May which marked the first one-month U.S. farm trade deficit in almost thirty years.

It appears that the shift away from government subsidies to stabilize prices, begun in the 1930s, toward subsidized credit and tax incentives to increase production, begun in the 1970s, has failed the farmers.

These programs, in effect, drove farmers into specialized crop production, and into deeper and deeper debt for purchases of additional acreage and heavy equipment. Then, when the world fell into recession in the eighties, the value of the dollar soared, land values plummeted, and foreign markets dried up, many U.S. farmers, like many debtor nations, found themselves unable to repay their creditors. Meanwhile, thanks both to technological advancement and to the incentive provided by the high dollar, some third-world countries, formerly food importers, became agriculturally self-sufficient. Still others became food exporters, competing with the U.S., the world's largest exporter of food.

The result has been a harvest of ironies: record crops and successive food surpluses forcing U.S. prices (and farmers' incomes) down, while creating the additional problem of paying billions for food storage; record government subsidies for farmers (around $30 billion this year) in face of delayed debt repayment, compounding the federal deficit; and inevitably, fewer and fewer farmers.

Since 1980, the rate of farm population decline—a steady 1 million farmers per decade since World War II—has doubled. Simultaneously, agribusiness and farm-management companies have grown. Today nearly half of the nation's food comes from 4 percent of farms with $200,000 in sales; not exactly the "family farm." And lenders who foreclosed on smaller farmers have hired management companies to work their land in order to repay the debts outstanding, spawning the boom in land-management firms. The number of farms overseen by such companies is predicted to encompass one-quarter of the nation's cropland by 1991, at the present growth rate. Is this the direction we want agriculture to be going? Consider the recent purchase by Metropolital Life of the nation's largest farm management business, Farmers National Company in Omaha, which manages over one million acres of farmland.

Some analysts see no problem with the shrinking number of farmers or with the centralization of land in the hands of a few huge conglomerates. They argue that underlying the "crisis" is the governmental blunder of protectionism which has shielded farmers from the rigors of a free-market economy and undermined efficiency, all at unwarranted taxpayer expense. Farming, they say, is a business just like any other, and this situation calls for fewer farmers, more efficient farms, and production that matches, not exceeds, demand. All this could be accomplished by a self-regulating market economy without government controls.

However, behind the rhetoric of market efficiency lies the unacknowledged premise: if government policy created today's plight for the medium-sized farmer, it also created the opportunity seized by agribusiness. Could it undo both? Aside from the myriad questions a centralized farming economy must pose for Americans, changes in government subsidies could affect corporation-owned as well as family-owned farms.

How then should government policies be redirected? Should such policies foster a centralized business model or preserve small- and medium-size farms and the farm culture associated with them?

The U.S. Catholic bishops, writing in the food and agriculture section of their draft pastoral letter on the economy (chapter 5), reject the business model. "Farmers and farm workers are not just another category of business entrepreneurs and hired laborers," they say as they urge federal policymakers to give priority to family farmers with less than $200,000 in annual sales. The bishops suggest that government could:

• Limit income support payments to those farmers with genuine need. Most farmers are now eligible, and present payments tend to increase in proportion to acreage, benefiting most of the largest producers.

• Placing a ceiling on payments to any one producer, carefully thwarting the practice of some producers who divide large parcels of land into smaller units to collect multiple subsidies.

• Utilize mandatory production controls to reduce surpluses, thereby increasing prices and income to farmers.

• Close tax incentives for non-farmers seeking tax shelters. That means limiting the use of farm losses to reduce taxes on non-farm income; making capital depreciation on equipment follow rather than exceed the actual decline in value; removing tax subsidies on capital gains which encourage investments in farming equipment and land expansion.

Fortunately, the Tax Reform Bill does include several general proposals which also apply to farming, such as reducing losses from passive investments, more realistic depreciation rates, and taxing capital gains at the standard income rate. In addition, several bills in Congress look promising.

The Save the Family Farm Act, sponsored by Senator Tom Harkin (D-Iowa) and Representative Richard A. Gephardt (D-Missouri), is consonant with the goals of the bishops in two respects: the central priority of saving the family farm, and claiming the necessity of mandatory production controls. The bill's purpose is to cut production, and thereby reduce surpluses, raise prices and farmer income, while simultaneously decreasing government subsidies. Currently, taxpayers underwrite federal subsidies to farmers; under this bill, consumers would bear a 3-5 percent price increase at the grocery store instead. Whether these costs would cancel each other out is not certain. But the problems with the bill are obvious: prices, if driven up, would be uncompetitive on the world market which is one reason behind present federal subsidies; and cuts in production mean reducing farm acreage. That's bad news for one-third of the nation's family farmers already on the brink of bankruptcy. And while the bill calls for production limits of less than 35 percent for any single commodity, curbing to a degree reduced acreage, the effects of such a program seem uncertain at home and unrealistic abroad.

Senator Robert Dole (R-Kansas) has proposed an export subsidy program for corn, wheat, and soybeans that would work like current subsidies for cotton and rice. Shippers would sell products at world prices—about half U.S. prices—with the federal government paying shippers the difference. This plan resembles price supports to farmers, only here the incentive goes to shippers who must find markets for farmers' goods, benefiting them indirectly. This proposal addresses the international market dilemma. It does not address the taxpayers' burden or the specific plight of family farmers.

Perhaps only a combination of strategies will solve this complex conundrum: government policies coupled with farmers' cooperatives, diversified crops, and a recommitment to thrift even after existing farm debts are restructured. Nevertheless, two questions—apparently, but not inevitably representing conflicting interests—must be squarely faced. What kind of farmers and farm culture are we willing to support at home? How can our import/export policies cultivate continued agricultural self-sufficiency for nations abroad?

RISKY BUSINESS[4]

"Jewell and Gil Ivey are decent, hardworking people," says an ad for *Country*, a widely acclaimed movie about farm life in Iowa. "Their way of life is an American tradition—a tradition that is now threatened by government bureaucrats. . . ."

In its opening scenes, *Country* provided a tableau of rural life, and a portrait of people who have chosen a no-frills existence. These are people who are—in the exasperated words of Jewell Ivey—"doing the best we can." Most of all, *Country* is a story about people trying to cope with circumstances beyond their control. It is early autumn, and the Iveys have just been through a month and a half without rain. A storm that sweeps across their fields at harvest time threatens the crops that remain.

But when Gil Ivey learns that he is on a list of troubled debtors compiled by the Farmers Home Administration (FmHA), it is clear that the most threatening uncertainties are in the economic climate. Worried that the agency might call in their loan, the Iveys go to talk with the regional administrator. He reviews their loan, and then says, "You're losing money. You should start thinking about liquidating your assets." Stunned, Gil responds, "You know what farm life is like. You can't look at it in the short run. Farming is a way of life." But the banker has the last word. "No, Gil," he says leaning across the desk, "farming is a *business*."

[4]Reprint of a staffwritten article in *The Farm Crisis*. Reprinted by permission from *The Farm Crisis*, pp.10-15. 1986. Copyright © 1986 by the Domestic Policy Association.

A Special Kind of Business

That is one of the central questions in the debate over farm policy. Is it appropriate to regard agriculture as we would any other business? Or is it a special case that requires unusual treatment and extraordinary protection?

In *Country* and other accounts of the plight of today's farmers, farm policy and the "government bureaucrats" who preside over it are often portrayed as the villains of the piece. Yet for 50 years, the premise of the federal farm program has been that agriculture is *unlike* other businesses, that it deserves special intervention and protection of various kinds.

For many businesses, the government provides some assistance, such as small business loans, or import fees on foreign products to protect American manufacturers. But in no other business does it take such a central role as in agriculture. The government conducts agricultural research; it helps farmers by providing subsidized water and electricity; it offers not only subsidized loans, but also crop insurance and disaster relief. Most important, it supports the income of many farmers, and, for some crops, manipulates prices and production levels.

The government's role on the farm is as expensive as it is ambitious. A recent report from the Congressional Budget Office concluded that, by most measures, farmers received more federal assistance than any other sector of the economy. Under the new farm bill, the annual cost of the farm program over the next few years will be about $20 billion.

What is the justification for federal assistance to farmers on that scale? The answer, quite simply, is that farming is a peculiarly risky business and a uniquely important one. The farm program's underlying assumption has been that the best way to sustain agricultural production is to provide a stable market, even if that means paying subsidies to farmers who are not economically distressed. To many of the defenders of the farm program, that rationale is at least as convincing today as it was half a century ago, when the federal farm program was first designed.

Some of the scenes in *Country*—farmers fighting back angry tears, auctioneers selling off farm equipment—look like film clips from the 1920s and 1930s, when plummeting farm prices combined with drought and dust storms to play havoc with the rural economy. One of the lessons of that wrenching experience was that if the farm economy is guided chiefly by the "invisible hand" of the free market, it will be poorly guided. Agriculture needs a moderating hand to smooth out cycles that otherwise would destroy even the best farmers.

In 1933, the Roosevelt administration introduced the first major farm legislation, called the Agricultural Adjustment Act. Under the terms of that act, producers of many crops—including wheat, corn, cotton, peanuts, tobacco, and rice—were required to reduce production in order to eliminate surpluses and increase prices. In return, the federal government agreed to keep farm prices up by buying certain crops when prices were low. The point of the program was to keep farmers in business despite temporary adversity, and thus to ensure a steady food supply to consumers.

Over the years, the farm program has changed in certain respects, but its rationale has remained intact. Then and now, the fundamental purpose of the nation's farm policy has been to help farmers cope with the capricious nature of the physical and economic environment. In the words of a recent report from the Senate Agriculture, Nutrition, and Forestry Committee, "The aim of federal farm policy is to induce elements of predictability into the inherently unpredictable business of farming."

When the farm bill was debated last year, some of the sharpest exchanges addressed the question of whether the government should continue to subsidize farmers by guaranteeing prices. Congressional defenders of price support programs made a point of reminding their colleagues that the hazards to which farmers have traditionally been exposed are still there. More so than other businessmen, as they pointed out, farmers are at the mercy of forces beyond their control.

Due to Circumstances beyond Our Control

Consider, for example, the extent to which farmers are vulnerable to the vicissitudes of nature. While today's farmers have some protection against crop disease, they are still vulnerable to hail, frost, and flooding. A few inches of rainfall during a growing season can mean the difference between a bumper crop and a very disappointing one. A few successive years of bad crops can mean the loss of a farm.

The unpredictability of the weather has far-reaching consequences that affect the prices at which farmers sell their products. In most industries, one can predict how much of a particular product is likely to be produced this year, and even a few years from now. Not so in farming. Next year could bring a record grain crop, causing prices to plummet. Or it could bring a failed wheat harvest, causing prices to soar. But there is no way of knowing these things in advance. Farmers have to plant their crops months before they have any idea how much demand there will be for them, and what price they are likely to command.

Fluctuations in the climate are just one of the uncertainties that makes farming a riskier business than most. Farmers also have to contend with substantial fluctuations in the market. The market for most agricultural commodities is characterized by sudden price shifts. In the three years from 1974 to 1977, for example, the price of wheat fell by 50 percent—the kind of shifts that is almost unheard of elsewhere. Most industries have a certain flexibility to respond to shifting markets. An auto manufacturer, for example, can close a plant, or lay off workers. But a farmer who has already planted a crop has few alternatives.

Unlike farmers, most producers are in a seller's market. They are in a position to determine the price they will charge for their product, and to make sure that it covers the costs of production plus a profit. But farmers cannot normally determine the price their products will command at market. Because the supply of food exceeds demand, individual farmers have little choice but to sell at whatever prices are offered. Consequently, in the words of John Adrian, a Kansas wheat farmer, "farm prices don't bear any relationship to the cost of production."

There is another factor that complicates things for the American farmer who sits down to calculate what he should grow, and tries to anticipate how profitable certain crops are likely to be. More than a third of all U.S. crops are harvested for export now, compared to less than one-fifth as recently as 1960. The expansion of overseas markets was a boon to American farmers in the 1970s. But it also made the job of predicting supply and demand more difficult. The economic well-being of American farmers now depends in large measure on dozens of unpredictable events in the international marketplace, such as the strength of the U.S. dollar and production decisions among farmers in Europe, South America, and Asia. Small variations in demand abroad can have a big effect on the prices American farmers get. In many ways, the farmer's fate is in the hands of others.

A Bread and Butter Industry

Ever since the 1930s, the farm program has been based upon the assumption that, because of their vulnerability to so many unpredictable events, farmers deserve special protection. Because of the unique importance of what is produced by this bread-and-butter industry, it is in the nation's interest to provide such assistance. In the words of Representative Dan Glickman (D-Kans.): "Farm policy ought to be considered in the same light as defense policy. You almost have to think of farmers as soldiers."

If our chief goal is to guarantee agricultural abundance, what kind of assistance is most appropriate? Since the Agricultural Adjustment Act was put into effect in the 1930s, the underlying assumption has been that the public is *not* well served by creating a special welfare program for troubled farmers. The aim of government-supported prices has been a stable farm market designed to keep the farm "factory" going at full throttle. These programs manipulate the supply, demand, and price of essential crops. For such a strategy to work, it has to apply not just to small or needy farmers, but to *all* farm producers. If only small farmers received price supports, the largest part of what is produced would still be subject to the fluctuations of the market.

Critics of farm price supports regard them not only as a very costly measure, but also as an indiscriminate handout to a great many farmers, no matter how wealthy. But farm lobbies that have advocated this approach justify subsidies as a way of ensuring farmers at least a minimal return. In their view, it is not in our interest to regard farm policy as a social policy whose goal is to keep every farmer in business, or to prevent population losses from rural areas. The nation is best served by farm programs whose chief goal is a sound farm *economy*. By continuing farm subsidies designed to stabilize prices and markets, we can help most farmers by maintaining a healthy farm economy. We should be less concerned about what kinds of units—large or small—the farm sector is comprised of, and more concerned about the farm sector's overall vitality.

Don't Knock Success

From this point of view, the important thing to remember about the farm program is that it has achieved its goal, which was to maintain agriculture's productive base, to provide adequate food supplies at a reasonable price, and to ensure most farmers a standard of living roughly equivalent to that enjoyed by most Americans. Proponents of this view feel that policies that pulled farmers out of the Great Depression and have kept American agriculture productive ever since are as appropriate now as they were in the past.

As Senator Quentin Burdick of North Dakota pointed out during the 1985 farm debate, it is ironic that the very success of this strategy has led to a situation in which many are complacent about the nation's ability to feed itself. "Just think of what our discussion would be today if we were talking about how to get into a position to feed ourselves. Instead, here we are spoiled by mountains of grain, and arguing about whether or not we should pull the rug out from under many of the people who contributed to our bounty."

Food in this country is actually quite cheap. Americans spend a smaller fraction of family income on food than people living in other industrial nations. "Commodity programs for farmers *are* costly," says Representative Wes Watkins (D-Okla.), "but I think we all have to agree that even though farmers have received subsidies in the past, the real beneficiary has been the consumer. I don't think any one of us would want to change a cheap food policy where only 16 percent of our disposable income is spent on food."

Even if you take into account the cost of farm subsidies which consumers pay through their taxes, that still adds only about 5 percent to current supermarket prices. To the proponents of continuing subsidy programs to many of the nation's farmers, this is the bottom line in the farm debate. With the government's assistance, the nation's farm system produces bountifully, and at modest prices. And that is sufficient reason to continue with the policy we have been pursuing. . . .

BLIND GENEROSITY[5]

If you travel around the country to places like Sioux Falls, South Dakota, where farm foreclosures have been occurring with numbing regularity, and ask farmers what they want, you hear a repeated refrain. "We don't want welfare," they say. "We want a fair price." The phrase is echoed on the placards displayed at farm rallies that have taken place on the steps of so many state capitols over the past few years. It is the same message that was heard in the halls of Congress this past year when "maintaining farm income" emerged as the battle cry of legislators who were trying to help struggling farmers.

It was the rationale for supporting farm prices and income at a cost of some $18 billion in 1985. The ambitious and increasingly costly price and income supports authorized by the 1985 farm bill represent the most recent step on a path this nation has been following since the 1930s.

Agricultural support programs were devised to respond to the problems of the Great Depression era. At a time when a far larger percentage of the population lived on farms, such programs were a major component of the New Deal relief effort. By subsidizing farm prices and income, the government helped farmers, most of whom were unarguably needy. "The farm programs with which we are familiar," explains Bob Bergland, who was Secretary of Agriculture in the Carter administration, "are rooted in the 1930s and based on the notion that all farms are alike, that benefits flow equally among all farms."

If the average farmer is a person of moderate means, operating a farm of moderate size, and he does not receive a fair income for his labor and investment, price supports can be justified as a way of ensuring farmers a fair return. But, as Bergland and others argue, in that assumption lies the key to understanding why today's farm policies do not work, and why we are paying so much for subsidies with so little apparent success. The farm program no longer meets its original objective of helping needy farmers by stabilizing their prices and income because the farm sector is different from what it was in the 1930s. As the people who take

[5]Reprint of a staffwritten article in *The Farm Crisis*. Reprinted by permission from *The Farm Crisis*, pp. 16-22. 1986. Copyright © 1986 by the Domestic Policy Association.

this position see it, subsidy programs intended for needy farmers have become an expensive and ill-targeted giveaway, and one that has the unfortunate effect of favoring large farms.

If the chief concern of the first position we examined is to maintain overall farm production, no matter what kinds of farms are required to do so, the emphasis of this second position is distinctly different. Its proponents feel that we should be concerned about maintaining a diverse farm sector that consists of smaller farms as well as large ones. They insist that the public interest is not well served by encouraging larger and larger farms. They advocate a different approach to providing assistance to farmers, one that provides help specifically to those who need it. To the people who take this position, it is essential to realize that there is no such thing as a "typical" farmer in the 1980s.

Gentlemen Farmers and Jolly Green Giants

To understand the farm sector is to come to terms with diversity. There are small farms and very large ones, and some in between—and the extremes are truly extreme.

Consider first the big farm producers. There are some 112,000 farms in this category, each of which grosses over $200,000 per year. They represent less than 5 percent of all farm operations, but they produce almost half of the national farm product. These are farms that have a heavy investment in land and equipment.

Chief among these green giants are the "superfarms." Less than 2 percent of all farm operators gross over $500,000 a year. In California's fertile Central Valley, for example, the biggest operator is a firm called Tenneco West Incorporated, which holds more than a million acres. In its management, and its use of capital and technology, it is an unmistakable instance of corporate agriculture.

At the other end of the scale are the small farm operations. In this category are about 1.5 million small farmers who account for only 12 percent of farm output. To call them farmers is to say more about where they reside than how they make their living. The owners of these operations earn an average of $18,000 a year, most of which is income from working full-time off the farm. The new small farmers, at least, are often gentlemen farmers who enjoy the agricultural life as a diversion, or "moonlighters" who work at agriculture as a second job.

Between these two extremes are some 520,000 farm operators whose gross income ranges from $40,000 to $200,000 per year. These farms are operated by proprietors who work the soil they own. Some operators of middle-sized farms are doing well financially, and moving up in size. Others, however, are struggling to stay in business, or resorting to off-farm employment to make ends meet.

Despite the diversity of the farm sector, virtually all farms are family-owned and operated. Since 97 percent of American farms are family farms, it is misleading to talk about saving family farming.

Who's in trouble? Not, by and large, the big farm operations, many of which are at least as profitable as commercial ventures in other sectors of the economy. Neither are the smallest farms in jeopardy. Since most of their owners' income derives from off-farm employment, they are in no immediate peril. In fact, in certain regions of the country, the number of small farmers has been increasing. In Vermont, farming is a favorite retreat for urban dwellers who want to get away from it all and claim certain tax advantages in the process.

It is the farmers in the middle, the full-time proprietor-operators, who are being squeezed out. By and large, they are the ones whose livelihood and way of life is endangered. As proponents of this second position see it, the reason why so many of them are in trouble has a lot to do with the nation's farm policy.

Welfare for the Wealthy

To its critics, the chief problem with the policy we have been pursuing is the criterion according to which subsidies are distributed. The underlying objective of the farm program—providing income support and protection to farmers—is similar to the objective of many social programs. Yet, there is an important difference in the way benefits are distributed. Through social programs such as Medicaid, Food Stamps, or Aid to Families with Dependent Children, we offer public assistance to help individuals. But the farm program rests upon quite a different principle. Subsidies are based on production, a simple dollars-per-bushel formula. The more you produce, the more you get. While a wheat farmer with 250 acres might get a support loan of $26,000, a farmer with 2,500 acres would get about 10 times as much.

While there is a nominal $50,000 limit to what farmers can get in deficiency payments, in practice there are few limits to what agricultural producers can get from the government.

The result, in the words of Representative Byron Dorgan (D-N.Dak.) is that "what began as survival programs for family farmers are becoming the domain of extra-large producers who often elbow aside the very family farmer for whom these programs were intended. . . . Those who produce the most get the most, and they need it least."

A recent study from the government's General Accounting Office shows where the federal farm subsidies are going. Almost 30 percent of all farm subsidies go to the largest 1 percent of all producers. Meanwhile, the 80 percent of all farmers with sales of less than $100,000 a year—the farms experiencing the greatest economic stress—receive less than a third of government payments. In brief, a small percentage of the nation's farmers, many of whom are doing quite well, get the bulk of government cash supports.

In the words of Assistant Secretary of Agriculture Robert L. Thompson, "What the farm income subsidies are really doing is transferring significant amounts of income to larger growers." To its critics, it amounts to a case of blindfolded generosity. Without regard to need, the government hands out farm subsidies not only to struggling farmers but also to million-dollar enterprises— and far more to the latter than to the former.

A Bias toward Bigness

The bias toward bigness that characterizes the nation's farm program is illustrated by what has happened to programs administered by the Farmers Home Administration (FmHA). The agency was created during the Great Depresssion as a lender of last resort, a banker for small farmers and those struggling to get their operations started. For years, the agency served its original purpose. Then, in the 1970s, Congress added a program called the Economic Emergency Loan Program. To qualify for it, you have to be in economic trouble, but you don't have to be small. Soon, the FmHA was lending far more in emergency assistance than in the kinds of loans for which the agency was established. In recent years, as Representative Dorgan points out, 90 percent of the agency's loans have gone to bigger, more established farms, many of which, in his words, are "unlikely candidates for public philanthropy." One politician and judge with an off-farm income of $70,000 and a net worth exceeding $400,000 received $266,000 from the government in such low-interest emergency loans.

As illustrated by the debate over the 1985 farm bill, the farm lobbies have seized upon well-publicized stories about the plight of failing farmers to justify extending the price and income support system. Yet, most of its benefits go to farmers who don't need help. Under the current program, for every one dollar of government subsidies that goes to a struggling farmer, some four dollars go to his more prosperous neighbor—who happens also to be his competitor.

Programs justified in the name of helping the "typical" farmer have done something else entirely. "What we have had," writes farm expert Willard Cochrane, "is a small group of aggressive farmers who, at the existing level of price and income supports, have made good profits. They have expanded their operations by acquiring the land and assets of their less capable neighbors. Government subsidies have increased their capacity to cannibalize the very farmers that the price and income supports were supposed to help. Meanwhile, most farm politicians and farm leaders have been standing on the sidelines, wringing their hands over the demise of the family farm."

It is a cruel irony. While distributing substantial subsidies to large farmers who are doing quite well, less than a quarter of the income and price support payments go to financially stressed farms. It is, writer Jonathan Rauch says, "among the most brutally inefficient welfare programs in the government—amounting to welfare, in many cases, for the wealthy." It is no coincidence, as proponents of this view see it, that medium-sized farms are increasingly being supplanted by larger ones, that large-scale farming is the fastest growing sector in the farm economy.

The important questions, as proponents of this view see it, are which farmers really deserve the government's help, and whether it is in the public interest to have a farm sector that consists mainly of large enterprises.

The Argument for Diversity

To critics of the current farm policy, a farm sector consisting of larger farms is not in the public interest. "I see no reason," says Willard Cochrane, "why taxpayers should provide an income subsidy to large farms. Nor do I believe that taxpayers should be required to pay for programs that help concentrate resources in the hands of fewer farmers and larger farms."

Some assume that bigger farms are more efficient and therefore represent our best bet to achieve further gains in productivity. Yet studies have shown that bigger farms are *not* inherently more efficient. A study conducted in 1979 by the USDA concluded that the average farm reaches 90 percent of its maximum efficiency at a size just over 300 acres. Beyond that, farms don't get more efficient, they just get bigger. The greater purchasing power of large farms allows them to buy supplies at lower prices, and so gives them a competitive advantage over smaller operations. But the most important reason why large farms have been gaining the upper hand is not that they are more efficient producers, but because they are favored by public policy. Their future depends upon special tax benefits and a continuing preference for subsidizing their farming methods rather than those of moderate-sized farms.

Concern about the increasing concentration in agriculture takes many forms. Some fear that if farm production becomes more centralized, a small number of owners will be in a position to monopolize food production and increase prices. Others are concerned that large farm operations are inflexible, incapable of responding to changes in demand. In the words of Representative Dorgan: "Just as a rope of many strands is more flexible and resilient than a single strand, a diverse agriculture of many relatively small units can adjust and change. Unlike the very largest operations, family farmers don't have so much capital tied up in what they did yesterday to keep them from doing what needs to be done tomorrow."

But the chief concern about what we lose when factory-in-the-field agglomerations gobble up smaller farms focuses on their social impact, not their economic consequences. In the 1940s, a researcher named Walter Goldschmidt carried out a study for the Department of Agriculture in which he examined the relationship between the scale of farm operations and community well-being. He compared two rural California communities, which were alike except that one, Dinuba, was made up mainly of moderate-sized farms, while the other, Arvin, was surrounded by large farms. When this study of the social and economic characteristics of the two towns was commissioned, it was assumed that it would show that bigger is better. But, to the contrary, Goldschmidt showed that Dinuba was a healthier community. It was more stable, had more small businesses, enjoyed a higher standard of living, better community facilities and more citizen participation.

By comparison, in Arvin the quality of life was adversely affected by the dominance of a small number of large farm enterprises. A community consisting of 20 large farms is different from one consisting of 200 smaller ones. Not only are fewer combines and silos purchased, there are also fewer homes, schools, and community groups. When farm operations are owned by large firms or land management companies, neither shareholders nor upper-level managers live in the region, and concern for the community diminishes.

As critics of the trend toward a smaller number of large farm operations see it, we have a choice between rural communities like Dinuba or Arvin. If medium-sized farmers continue to go out of business, we risk the loss of entire communities, indeed the loss of a way of life.

Speaking to his congressional colleagues during the debate over the 1985 farm bill, Senator James Abdnor (R-S.Dak.) said: "I want to alert you to a clear and present danger, an America without agriculture the way we have known it. If we fail with agriculture, we will have a rural America without economic purpose and an America without its heritage. The continued failure of our farmers, our rural bankers, our Main Street merchants will ripple disastrously through the fabric of national life for generations to come."

Helping Needy Farmers

From this perspective, it is not advisable to move any farther in the direction of a farm sector dominated by a small number of large producers. Our chief goal should be to help needy farmers. By that criterion, the current policy leaves a lot to be desired. The new farm bill actually increases the amounts big farmers can get from federal programs, thereby inviting further consolidation of farms.

To reverse course, and move in the direction of a diverse farm sector, several steps should be taken. As a first step, blatant abuses should be corrected. The 1985 farm bill added yet more exceptions to the rules that limit the benefits of federal programs to large farmers. Proponents of this view are convinced that this is not the direction in which we should be moving.

If we are serious about maintaining a diverse farm sector, fundamental changes in policy are needed. Benefits should be targeted specifically to small and medium-sized commercial farmers. This assistance could take many forms, including management assistance and additional low-interest farm loans. The FmHA loan program should be restored to its original purpose of helping beginning and smaller farmers. Additionally, tax laws should be altered to eliminate practices that are detrimental to small farmers, such as laws that invite farm investment as a tax shelter, thus driving up land prices and discouraging beginning farmers.

In particular, if we are serious not only about keeping as many farmers on the land as possible but also about reducing government expenditures, the entire system of price supports should be eliminated. A program whose purpose and original intention are so seriously at odds with its actual results deserves to be discarded.

Eliminating the main programs by which government has assisted farmers for the past half-century is a drastic action. Particularly at a time when the farm economy is depressed, and when many farmers are going out of business, doing so would put an additional strain on farmers who are already stretched to the limit. Yet proponents of this second choice feel it is the right action to take. What farmers who are overburdened with debt really need is not expanded price supports—which offer less to endangered farmers than to their prosperous neighbors—but special credit programs that substantially reduce the interest rates they are obliged to pay.

Most of all, we should turn an implicit and ineffective welfare program for farmers into an explicit, well-targeted, and effective welfare program for those who need assistance. There is a reason why, among the various farm proposals considered by Congress this past year, no one proposed a means test for farm subsidies. Because farmers don't want to be on the dole, that is still widely regarded as politically impractical. But proponents of this position are convinced that giving subsidies directly to needy farmers makes a lot more sense than linking subsidies to production levels.

Since farms vary so much from one region to another, and according to the crops in which they specialize, targeting benefits to farms that need and deserve assistance would be no easy task. But this represents a far more promising way to promote efficient commercial farms in a variety of sizes, including the small to medium-sized farms.

Hybrid Vigor

The people who look at the farm problem from this perspective are concerned about what *kinds* of farms receive government subsistence, and about maintaining the diversity of the farm sector. Largely because of subsidy programs that offer across-the-board benefits to many farmers, our policy has inadvertently favored large-scale, factory-in-the-field operations. It has been a very costly program, and one that has led to the destruction of more modest farm operations.

Farm policy should reflect a social value—the importance we attach to a rural America that consists of small and medium-sized farmers as well as large producers. Proponents of this position would use the government's farm policy as a tool to stop the further erosion of smaller farms, to keep many of the farmers in business who are now having so much trouble making ends meet. . . .

FARMERS, MARKETS, AND PROFITS[6]

In 1984, when the film *Country* was released, some commentators were less than enthusiastic about it. The film was intended as a sympathetic portrait of a beleaguered farm family, an appeal for greater support—particularly from the "government bureaucrats" who were about to foreclose on the Iveys' loan. But

[6]Reprint of a staffwritten article in *The Farm Crisis*. Reprinted by permission from *The Farm Crisis*, pp. 23-28. 1986. Copyright © 1986 by the Domestic Policy Association.

as the *New Republic*'s columnist TRB wrote, the film unintention-
ally provided something else entirely.

"*Country* does tell an all-American story," he writes, "though
not the one its producers think. Like most Americans, farmers
imagine they want the government to get off their backs. But no
group is more coddled by government than farmers, and none is
more whiny and self-pitying. If, after getting subsidized research
and development, subsidized electricity, subsidized crop insurance, subsidized water, subsidized storage, subsidized export promotion, and above all, subsidized price supports, the Iveys still
cannot pay off their subsidized low-interest government loans,
the government is *entitled* to collect its collateral, even if this
means putting the Iveys out of the farming business."

There we are, in the columnist's words, "pulling out our han-
kies for Gil Ivey"—all the while paying through the nose to
support him. Just a few months earlier, as TRB recalls, the Administration appealed for the support of farmers, taking credit
for providing them with more than $35 billion in federal re-
sources. The government spends more on programs for farmers
than it does on Medicaid and Food Stamps put together. It is a
fine example of misplaced priorities, of not putting resources
where they are needed. And government support for farmers has
been growing even faster than defense spending.

As the column concludes, "It is not merely that the government wastes a lot of money on agriculture—billions to increase
production, then billions more to reduce production and/or dis-
pose of the excess—but that the whole extravaganza takes place
in a political never-never land, unconsciously well captured in
Country, where the beneficiaries think they are rugged individual-
ists in the best American tradition."

This is quite a different perspective not only on *Country* but
also on the farm crisis and what should be done about it. To the
people who share this perspective, the farm program is a conspic-
uous example of where our sympathies have led us to the creation
of a policy that is neither sensible nor workable.

This view shares many of the concerns of the first two positions we examined. Its proponents recognize that farmers are
suffering because their income has declined. But far from concluding that increased government subsidies might solve the
problem, people who take this position are convinced that government intervention itself is the farmer's largest handicap, and

that market-oriented policies must be the foundation for a successful strategy to restore prosperity to the nation's farmers.

Who's to Blame?

Farm profits have shrunk for each of the past four years, and many of the nation's farmers are insolvent. But who's to blame? In large part, as those who take this perspective see it, farmers themselves deserve much of the blame, especially the "plungers" who are being foreclosed on for loans they should never have taken out in the first place.

In the words of former Secretary of Agriculture John Block, an Illinois hog farmer: "We in agriculture built our own trap. We're all responsible: the farmers who bid up the land; the so-called experts who said, 'Buy another piece of land—they ain't making any more of it'; the lending institutions that couldn't shovel the money out the door fast enough. We all fell into the trap and expanded too much and too fast."

The essence of the free enterprise system is that entrepreneurs can reap the benefits of a wise investment. By the same token, they also take a risk. If a business becomes unprofitable because its owner takes on too much debt or orders merchandise that doesn't sell, the government bears no responsibility for keeping the business going. It steps in only to provide a procedure for bankruptcy, and to offer unemployment compensation to ease employees' transition into another job. In the short run, it is unfortunate and no doubt painful when a firm goes out of business. But over the long run, such adjustments are not only necessary but desirable. That is how the "invisible hand" of the market adjusts supply to demand.

Those who would reduce the government's role in agriculture recall the premise of our economic system. In the economic realm, as in others, government governs best when it governs least. To ensure the long-term health of the farm economy, the government should stay out of it as much as possible. It's not fair, they feel, to allow farmers the rewards of free enterprise while protecting them from the risks, unless we're prepared to do the same for other businesses. That was former director of the Office of Management and Budget David Stockman's point when he said, "For the life of me, I can't figure out why taxpayers should be expected to refinance bad debt willingly incurred by consenting adults who went out and bought farmland when prices were going up and thought they could get rich."

Welfare for Farmers

If farmers themselves are partly to blame for the farm crisis, so too is government. "For the past 50 years," as John Block puts it, "government has been trying to protect farmers into prosperity and profitability. And what do we have to show for all this help? We have a weakened agricultural sector that lurches from crisis to crisis, from Band-Aid to Band-Aid."

The government has set up various programs to insulate farmers from the market. The result, many feel, is an illogical system that fails both as economic and social policy.

That hasn't always been the case. Abraham Lincoln first proposed an agriculture department to Congress back in 1862, when some four out of five Americans lived on the farm. When Lincoln made the proposal, he applauded the nation's farmers as "a great interest so independent in its nature as to not have demanded and extorted more from government." In its first year, the Agriculture Department, whose initial task was to distribute seeds to farmers, had a staff of nine and a budget of $64,000.

What began as a modest effort to assist farmers has grown dramatically. Initially, aid was targeted on the basis of hardship or national purpose. Over the years, many of the programs lost their original focus but gained political support. Because farmers make up a substantial proportion of the population in rural communities, they can make powerful claims on the legislature. Consequently, farmers' interests are well represented in Washington, and programs that amount to little more than an entitlement for particular farm groups have been maintained and expanded.

To critics of the government's farm program, dairy policy provides a clear example of what has gone wrong. Dairy interests are the farm community's most powerful lobbyists in Washington. For some years, both the support price for milk and the dairy diversion program—in which the government pays farmers not to produce—have been sacrosanct. In 1985, government support for dairy farmers cost about $1.6 billion. This amounts to a costly incentive to overproduction.

Welfare programs are criticized when they don't solve the problems they were intended to cure. Yet there has been relatively little public complaint about farm programs that offer what amounts to a welfare program for farmers. By 1989, it is estimated that farmers will depend on Uncle Sam for more than 70 percent of their net income, up from about 25 percent in 1984. It is a sure sign, say critics, that we are on the wrong path.

Mountains of Grain, Rivers of Milk

It is particularly troubling that federal policies exacerbate the problem by stimulating even more farm production. In other industries, when too much of a certain product is produced, falling prices relay a signal back to the producers. If lower prices don't attract more customers, some producers cut back on production, and others go out of business altogether. Gradually, the surplus is reduced as supply adjusts to demand.

But in the farm market, those signals are obscured by the government's presence. When demand is low, the government buys the surplus to keep prices up. Since the government is willing to buy at higher prices, farmers have no incentive to sell on the market at a lower price or to cut back on production. Food is thus produced expressly for sale to Uncle Sam.

It is not surprising, then, that the government ends up with a well-stocked larder. The extent of surplus farm products bought by the government each year is staggering. In 1985, farm products owned by the federal government were valued at $6.9 billion. This included 2.6 billion pounds of dairy products in the form of butter, cheese, and dried milk, 500 million bushels of wheat, 143,000 bales of cotton and 140 million pounds of honey. It costs us almost $400 million a year just to store those surpluses. Despite the fact that the 1985 farm bill lowered the level of price supports to encourage farmers to sell to the market, the amount of grain in U.S. stockpiles is headed for another all-time record this year.

There are various reasons why Americans farms have become more productive. Due to selective breeding, growth hormones and better diet, the average cow now produces twice as much as its forebear did 20 years ago. With new hybrids and chemicals coming onto the market, farm productivity can be expected to rise in any case.

But government policy has contributed to the problem of overproduction. Consider, for example, what happens when a farm such as the Ivey's is foreclosed. The land is sold, in many cases to the neighboring farmer, who puts it back into production, knowing that if there is no market for the additional product, the government will buy it. Because of the government's role, this cycle of foreclosure, purchase, and production by a different owner does nothing to correct the underlying problem.

Some programs attempt to solve the problem by offering incentives to reduce acreage under cultivation. But others encourage greater crop production. For example, the government subsidizes irrigation, thus allowing the cultivation of areas that were not formerly arable. The government also offers tax shelters to encourage such activities as feeding facilities for cattle and hogs, and the planting of vineyards and orchards. As critics see it, that is a blatant contradiction. From one pocket, the government hands out tax breaks to encourage farm investment. From the other, it hands out subsidies to compensate farmers for the depressed prices that result from overproduction. By encouraging overproduction, one part of our farm policy creates the very problem that another part seeks to solve. To proponents of this view, it doesn't make sense and it shouldn't continue.

Propping Up the Losers

Another problem arises when government offers subsidies or loans that allow marginal farmers to stay in business. Writer Gregg Easterbrook explains why propping up the losers is the wrong thing to do by imagining what would happen if the government intervened in the computer industry, which is also plagued by overproduction. "Suppose the government stepped into the computer industry," he writes, "to make sure no manufacturer went out of business. Successful companies like IBM and Apple would be unhappy, because the artificial stimulation of supply would prevent them from getting full value for their products. Unsuccessful companies would find themselves in the debilitating position of being dependent on Uncle Sam and ridden with anxiety over whether their handouts would continue. Everybody would be working, yet no one would be happy. There would be a 'computer crisis.'"

That is just what the government has done in agriculture. In the long run, no one benefits from fabricating demand where no true demand exists. What is most unfortunate about such a policy is that it can make losers out of farmers who might have succeeded in a free market.

That is why proponents of this position conclude that government management of agriculture is both unfair and unsound. Two-thirds of American farmers make money without government subsidies. We would have a far healthier farm economy if the rest learned to do the same, or went into another business.

World Markets for a World-Class Producer

In their view, the only realistic way to enhance farmers' income—and the income of food processors, packagers, and wholesalers—is to build demand for American products. America is uniquely blessed with rich farmland, good weather, an efficient transportation system and superior technology. These give us a natural advantage, a competitive edge over farm producers worldwide. There is no reason why American farmers can't continue to provide not only for domestic food needs but also for a larger portion of the world food market. The best solution to the problem of "oversupply" is to expand our markets, to make a more aggressive effort to sell agriculture products abroad.

Exports are the lifeblood of American agriculture. With the produce from one in every three acres going overseas, the export market is crucial to the success of the nation's farmers. For some crops, an even higher percentage goes to foreign markets. In 1981, for example, fully half of the soybeans and three-fifths of the wheat grown by American farmers was for export.

Total agricultural export revenues in 1981, when farmers sent a record 162 million metric tons abroad, were a whopping $44 billion. As it happens, this nation's fortunes as a food exporter have been declining ever since. In each of the past four years, the volume of exports has decreased, sinking to 126 million metric tons in 1985. In fact, farm products now make up less than 14 percent of the value of all American exports, the lowest level since 1940.

Why have American farmers been losing ground in the international market? Here too, proponents of a market-oriented policy are convinced that government interference is to blame. The nation's farm program, especially its price supports, prices American farmers out of the international market. To advocates of a market-oriented policy, the 1985 farm bill represented a step in the right direction. It cut price supports in an effort to make American farm goods competitive with those produced in other countries. To the proponents of a market-oriented farm policy, an aggressive effort to regain a larger share of the foreign market is the best hope for American agriculture, the most promising way to enhance farm income.

Too Many Farms, Too Many Farmers

Sometimes it is easier to see what is in the public interest by looking at what was done in the past, and examining its results. The people who propose a market-oriented farm policy point to the long-term decline in the number of farmers, and insist that it's a good thing that it happened. Higher productivity by a smaller number of farmers is a good measure of increasing efficiency and productivity. If assistance had been offered to every troubled farmer in the 1930s, when more than one in four Americans lived on farms, today's economy would be far less productive. But the farm exodus continued at relatively high levels even into the 1950s and 1960s. In 1951, for example, the number of farms declined by 220,000; in 1961 by 138,000. Yet here we are, at a time when the number of farms declines by only 40,000 or so each year, considering bailouts to prevent a painful but necessary process. This nation would be better off with fewer farms and fewer farmers.

What we should fear is not a market that adjusts to changing circumstances by putting people and capital to better use, but a political process that responds to immediate distress with decisions that are in no one's long-term interest. In the midst of debate over the 1985 farm bill, Representative Kika de la Garza of Texas, chairman of the House Agriculture Committee, said he might support certain changes in the farm program, but only if they could be accomplished "without sacrificing a single farmer." As writer Gregg Easterbrook comments, "That is like saying, 'Let's cut back the bloated defense budget—as long as no contractors lose work.'"

Here, as elsewhere, there is a cost to each policy we might pursue. One of the costs of moving toward a more prudent farm policy is that some farmers and their families will have to find other employment. Government should not stand in the way of the process.

If it is appropriate to be more charitable to farmers than to other displaced workers—an assumption that many advocates of a market orientation reject—extraordinary measures could be taken to ease their transition into nonfarm employment. The state of Nebraska, for example, has been running a program called "Farmers in Transition" since 1984, which provides ex-farmers with job training and placement services. That modest effort provides an example of what can be done for farmers when it no longer makes sense for them to stay in agriculture.

One writer, James Bovard, proposes a more radical effort along those lines. He advocates generous incentives to persuade marginal farmers to move to other lines of employment. As Bovard suggests, "Instead of paying perpetual bonuses for not producing, the government should offer struggling full-time farmers a one-time severance payment. In return for hanging up his plow, every farmer with a net worth of less than $50,000 could be given up to $50,000 to help start a new life. This would provide a humanitarian transition and cost relatively little. After this generous bailout, there would be no excuse for crafting agriculture policy as if most farmers were widows and orphans. There would be a shakeout. But it would be far cheaper over the long run than continuing to gold plate every granary in the land."

Free Markets

From this perspective, the debate over the future of America's farms is about whether government or free markets do a better job of guiding farm production. Despite unprecedented government subsidies, the farm sector is in severe distress. To many that is a clear indication of what should be done. "We can't continue with a farm policy built on false hopes and high dependence on the government," says former Secretary of Agriculture John Block. "Agriculture will be better off with a farm policy that lets the market system work."

What role should the government play? Few people would completely eliminate the government's role in agriculture. Even among those convinced of the value of a market-oriented farm economy, there is general support, for example, for a continued government role in agricultural research. But it is clear what the government should *not* do. It shouldn't offer incentives to overproduction. It shouldn't imperil the farmer's ability to compete in international markets. And it shouldn't do anything that is contrary to the interest of the most efficient producers. . . .

BIBLIOGRAPHY

An asterisk (*) preceding a reference indicates that the article or part of it has been reprinted in this book.

BOOKS AND PAMPHLETS

Bergland, Bob, ed. A time to choose: summary report on the structure of agriculture. U.S. Department of Agriculture. '81.

Berry, Wendell. The unsettling of America: culture and agriculture. Sierra. '77.

Bhagat, Shantilal P. The family farm: can it be saved? Brethren. '85.

*The Farm Crisis. Domestic Policy Association. '86.

Goldschmidt, Walter. As you sow. Allenheld, Osmun. '78.

MacFayden, J. Tevere. Gaining ground: the renewal of America's small farms. Ballantine Books. '85.

Malcolm, Andrew. Final harvest. Times Press. '86.

Martin, Henry. Farm exports; what's happening to our foreign markets. RRN Books. '83

Marton, Larry B., ed. United States agriculture in a global economy: agriculture yearbook, nineteen eighty-five. U.S. Government Printing Office. '85.

Poirot, Paul L., ed. The farm problem. Freeman. '86.

Thompson, Roger. Farm finance: deepening debt crisis. Editorial Research Reports. '86.

Williams, Simon and Karen, Ruth. Agribusiness and the small-scale farmer. Westview. '85.

PERIODICALS

The plight of the farmers. America. 152:226-27. Mr. 23, '85.

*How we're gonna keep 'em off of the farm. Mueller, William. American Scholar. 56:57-67. Winter '87.

*Making sense of agriculture. Easterbrook, Gregg. Atlantic. 256:63-78. Jl. '85.

Down on the farm; new legislation is apt to hit agriculture hard. Tucker, William. Barron's. 65:30. Je. 21, '85.

*Playing with fire: Reagan takes on the American farmer. Crawford, Mark H. Business Week. pp. 60-61. Ja. 14, '85.

A farm slump that betters futures traders, too. Frank, John N. Business Week. pp. 75-76. F. 4, '85.

How the farm credit crisis is crushing America's breadbasket. Pollock, Michael A. Business Week. 124:26. F. 18, '85.

Farm supports: start dismantling. Editorial. Business Week. p. 162. F. 18, '85.

Homemade tonics for the farm crisis. Business Week. p. 36. Mr. 11, '85.

The farm rut gets deeper. Frank, John N., et al. Business Week. pp. 32-33. Je. 17, '85.

The good earth is bad news. Houston, Patrick, et al. Business Week. pp. 30-31. Ag. 19, '85.

The credit crisis isn't staying down on the farm. Houston, Patrick, et al. Business Week. pp. 90-91. S. 30, '85.

The farm crisis has financially migrated to California. Toy, Stewart, et al. Business Week. pp. 116-17. O. 28, '85.

Why the farm crisis goes on and on. Editorial. Business Week. p. 152. N. 25, '85.

Hard times will get harder down on the farm. Houston, Patrick. Business Week. pp. 76-77. Ja. 13, '86.

A grim harvest for the nation's farm banks. Pitzer, Mary J. Business Week. p. 77. Ja. 13, '86.

America's deflation belt. Business Week. p. 52. Je. 9, '86.

Farmers will reap a bumper crop of supports. Pollock, Michael A. Business Week. p. 83. Ja. 12, '87.

A bushel of farm debt lands on Congress. Smart, Tim. Business Week. p. 44. Mr. 16, '87.

In the farm belt, the worst is over. Smart, Tim. Business Week. pp. 46-47. My. 18, '87.

A farm proposal. Challenge. 28:54+. Jl./Ag. '85.

Agriculture and political economy. Challenge. 28:15+ N./D. '85.

*America's farmers: desperate in the Midwest. Woodward, Judith L. Christian Century. 102:372. Ap. 17, '85.

Facing up to the farm crisis. Rebeck, Victoria. Christian Century. 104:381-83. Ap. 22, '87.

Depression comes to small farm towns. Christian Science Monitor. p. 1. Ja. 7, '86.

Preserving an agrarian heritage. Editorial. Christian Science Monitor. p. 5. My. 7, '86.

*Which future for farming? Editorial. Commonweal. 113:547-48. O. 24, '86.

A bumper crop: American farm subsidies. Learn, Elmer W., et al. Current. 288:4-10. D. '86.

Farm crisis: the worst is yet to come. Dun's Business Month. 218:41. S. '86.

Broken heartland. Bauer, Douglas. Esquire. 107:68–77. Ja. '87.

Deflation in the farm belt. Bladen, Asby. Forbes. 135:196. F. 25, '85.

Down on the farm—unwillingly. Simon, Ruth. Forbes. 137:40+. Je. 16, '86.

Some problems won't go away. Flint, Jerry. Forbes. 138:74–78. S. 22, '86.

Getting Uncle Sam off the farm. Worthey, Ford S. Fortune. 111:128–32. Mr. 18, '85.

Facts vs. the furor over farm policy. Ehrbar, Aloysius. Fortune. 112:114–18+. N. 11, '85.

Holding to the land. Beer, Ralph. Harper's. 27:57–64. S. '85.

Should Uncle Sam save the American farmer? Shilling, A. Gary. Los Angeles Times. Sec. VI. p. 3. F. 24, '85.

25% of state farms may face bankruptcy. Los Angeles Times. Sec. IV, p. 3. O. 3, '85.

House passes farm bill keyed to price supports. Los Angeles Times. Sec. I. p. 1. O. 9, '85.

Seeds of discontent: Iowa's farm-based economy is ill, worsening. Los Angeles Times. Sec. IV, p. 1. Je. '87.

Trouble on tobacco road. Maclean's. 97:47. Jl. 30, '84.

The squeeze on indebted farmers. Moir, Garry. Maclean's. 98:17–19. Mr. 4, '85.

Timely aid for the farm belt. McDonald, Marci. Maclean's. 98:22. Mr. 11, '85.

A hard luck harvest. Barrett, Cindy. Maclean's. 98:22. O. 28, '85.

The South's deadly drought. Maclean's. 98:22. O. 28, '85.

*Blowing away the family farmer. Ball, Heather and Beatty, Leland. Nation. 239:442–4. N. 3, '84.

Farm protests hit the state houses. Schwab, Jim. Nation. 240:42–44. Ja. 19, '85.

*A farm bill by and for farmers. Lanner, Devorah. Nation. 241:19–20. Jl. 6, '85.

Singing for AID. Nation. 241:300. O. 5, '85.

Farm credit bailout; saving the system, not the farmers. Nation. 242:44–46. Ja. 18, '86.

*Broken heartland. McBride, Bob. Nation. 242:132–33. F. 8, '86.

*The rise of the rural ghetto. Davidson, Osha. Nation. 242:820–21. Je. 14, '86.

Farm blues. McLaughlin, John. National Review. 37:24. Mr. 22, '85.

1½ cheers for David Stockman. Hyde, Henry J. National Review. 37:26–28. Je. 28, '85.

Agriculture: no turnabout. Eason, Henry. Nation's Business. 74:68. Ja. '86.

*The idiocy of rural life. Pasley, Jeffrey L. New Republic. 195:24–27. D. 8, '86.

Rising suicides in farm belt reflect surge in hardship and despondency. New York Times. p. A 11. Ja. 14, '86.

If family farms are to survive, Reagan must end his 'free market' policy. New York Times. p. 21. S. 22, '86.

Georgia farm despair stokes anger at G. O. P. New York Times. p. A 14. S. 26, '86.

Foreclosed farms being sold as land values start to rise. New York Times. p. A 1. My. 1, '87.

Bitter fight over the farms. Newsweek. 105:17. Mr. 4, '85.

A bumper crop of problems. McCormick, John. Newsweek. 106:60. Jl. 15, '85.

New twist in a farm crisis. Pauly, David. Newsweek. 106:60. S. 16, '85.

For farmers, the fill is due. Newsweek. 107:45. Ja. 13, '86.

Farmer's barnyard blues. Pauly, David. Newsweek. 108:38. Ag. 4, '86.

Welfare for farmers? Newsweek. 108:12. S. 22, '86.

The heretics of the heartland. McCormick, John. Newsweek. 109:46. Mr. 30, '87.

Farms: the bulls rush in. Quinn, Jane Bryant. Newsweek. 109:48. Je. 22, '87.

The trouble on the land. Progressive. 49:11. Ap. '85.

The farmer in the cell. Kobat, Paul. Progressive. 49:50. N. '85.

*Plowed under. Brodner, Steve. Progressive. 51:35–40. My. '87.

*A bumper crop: American farm subsidies. Learn, Elmer W., et al. The Public Interest. pp. 66–78. Summer '86.

*U.S. farm dilemma: the global bad news is wrong. Avery, Dennis. Science. 230:408–12. O. 25, '85.

The grim yield of modern farming. Mueller, William. Sierra. 70:44–45. My./Je. '85.

Rent trouble on the farm. Time. 125:24–8. F. 18, '85.

I will veto again and again. Time. 125:24. Mr. 18, '85.

The new grapes of wrath. Greenwald, John. Time. 125:66–67.

Bountiful harvest, bleak outlook. Rudolph, Barbara. Time. 126:44. Ag. 26, '85.

Hat in hand. Time. 126:71. N. 11, '85.

Amber waves of debt. Time. 127:67. Mr. 3, '86.

Cries of the heart. Sidey, Hugh. Time. 128:15. Ag. 11, '86.

Too much of a good thing. Time. 128:22. S. 8, '86.

America's farmers down the tubes? Sheets, Kenneth R. U.S. News & World Report. 98:47–49. F. 4, '85.

It looks pretty bleak for a lot of farmers. U.S. News & World Report. 98:63–64. F. 18, '85.

Farmers up in arms. U.S. News & World Report. 98:22–29. Mr. 11, '85.

Banks, too, hit hard by rural woes. Scherschal, Patricia M. U.S. News & World Report. 98:29. Mr. 11, '85.

Few hopes blossom for farmers in spring of '85. Sheets, Kenneth R. U.S. News & World Report. 98:74–75. My. 20, '85.

Ailing farm economy—damage spreads wide. Sheets, Kenneth R. U.S. News & World Report. 99:53–54. Jl. 29, '85.

A bountiful harvest that's hard to swallow. Sheets, Kenneth R. U.S. News & World Report. 99:82–83. N. 11, '85.

*Family life takes beating in farm crisis. Bosc, Michael. U.S. News & World Report. 99:62. N. 18, '85.

Winter of despair hits the farm belt. Huntley, Steve. U.S. News & World Report. 100:21–23. Ja. 20, '86.

The South's new grapes of wrath. U.S. News & World Report. 101:6. S. 1, '86.

Learning to survive on the land. Bosc, Michael. U.S. News & World Report. 102:30. F. 2, '87.

What's to become of the American farm? USA Today (magazine). 115:10–28. Jl. '86.

Farm program spending to rise to record in '86. Wall Street Journal. p. 6. F. 24, '86.

Farmers likely to idle more land in '86. Wall Street Journal. p. 32. Mr. 17, '86.

Many farmers have it rough but the economy will survive. Clark, Lindley H. Wall Street Journal. p. 31. Mr. 25, '86.

Farm optimism rises, but woes persist. Wall Street Journal. p. 4. My. 11, '87.

No bailout for farmers, Reagan says. Washington Post. p. A 1. F. 24, '85.

U.S. farm population shows decline. Washington Post. p. 19. Ja. 16, '86.

Administration would tighten rules for receiving farm subsidies. Sinclair, Ward. Washington Post. p. A 13. Mr. 15, '87.

Grief is growing in the farm land. Sinclair, Ward. Washington Post. p. A 3. My. 24, '87.

U.S. farm debt bomb. World Press Review. 32:70–72. F. '85.